From Daughters
to Disciples

From Daughters to Disciples

Women's Stories from the New Testament

Lynn Japinga

WESTMINSTER
JOHN KNOX PRESS
LOUISVILLE · KENTUCKY

First edition
Published by Westminster John Knox Press
Louisville, Kentucky

21 22 23 24 25 26 27 28 29 30—10 9 8 7 6 5 4 3 2 1

Book design by Drew Stevens
Cover design by Barbara LeVan Fisher, www.levanfisherdesign.com
Cover art: Black Madonna*, 2004 (woodcut print in oils), James, Laura (Contemporary Artist) /*
Private Collection / Bridgeman Images

Library of Congress Cataloging-in-Publication Data
Names: Japinga, Lynn, 1960- author.
Title: From daughters to disciples : women's stories from the New Testament
/ Lynn Japinga.
Description: First edition. | Louisville, Kentucky : Westminster John Knox
Press, 2021. | Includes index. | Summary: "In this second of two
volumes, Lynn Japinga acquaints readers with the women of the Bible.
This Bible study introduces and retells every female character who
contributes to one or more New Testament stories, diving deeply into
what each woman's story means for us today with questions for reflection
and discussion"-- Provided by publisher.
Identifiers: LCCN 2020047402 (print) | LCCN 2020047403 (ebook) | ISBN
9780664265700 (paperback) | ISBN 9781646980000 (ebook)
Subjects: LCSH: Bible. New Testament--Biography. | Women in the Bible. |
Bible. New Testament--Biography.
Classification: LCC BS2445 .J37 2021 (print) | LCC BS2445 (ebook) | DDC
225.9/22/082--dc23
LC record available at https://lccn.loc.gov/2020047402
LC ebook record available at https://lccn.loc.gov/2020047403

Most Westminster John Knox Press books are available at special quantity discounts when purchased in bulk by corporations, organizations, and special-interest groups. For more information, please e-mail SpecialSales@wjkbooks.com.

*In honor of Dr. Jane Bach, Dr. Jane Dickie,
and the Rev. Dr. Leonard Kalkwarf;
and in memory of the Rev. Dr. Wayne Boulton,
the Rev. Dr. Elton Bruins, and the Rev. Dr. Robert Palma
—teachers, mentors, friends.*

Contents

Acknowledgments

I am grateful to my students at Hope College, with whom I've been studying these texts for almost three decades. The stories provoke their anger, perplexity, curiosity, insights, and occasional delight. I appreciate their questions and their honesty.

Doug Van Aartsen carefully read the entire manuscript and offered many perceptive comments. Pamela Valkema proofread the final version. I am grateful for her sunny disposition, patience, and organizational skills. She makes my life easier. Ruth Lowry read several chapters and caught a number of errors. The members of the Religion Department at Hope College discussed two chapters at a colloquy meeting. Phil Munoa answered my questions about Greek.

I did not benefit from Kyle Dipre's rigorous editing because he was busy with life, love, and law school. He did read a couple of early chapters and was a constant source of encouragement.

Laurie Baron again served as my "book whisperer" with her intuitive and grace-filled editing and conversation.

The 8th Street McDonald's provided space where I could get something done when I was stalled out. The crew there tolerated my loitering, even beyond closing at times, and expressed interest in my work. I was and am graced by their kindness.

The librarians at Hope College and Western Theological Seminary were patient with my repeated renewals and requests for interlibrary loans.

Hope College funded a summer of research and writing with a Nyenhuis Faculty Development Grant.

I appreciate the editorial and production staff at Westminster John Knox Press. Their wisdom and attention to detail have saved me from many errors.

My parents, Roger and Wilma Winkels, and children, Mark Japinga and Annie and Jordan Carrigan, continue to be great sources of encouragement and support. My grand-dog Wrigley, on the other hand, offered no insight at all into the women of the New Testament and probably delayed the project with his requests for walks and attention, but he provided much needed exercise and delight.

This book is dedicated to Hope College professors Jane Bach, Wayne Boulton, Elton Bruins, Jane Dickie, and Robert Palma and to my seminary internship supervisor, Leonard Kalkwarf. They taught me how to be a teacher, a scholar, and a pastor. I am indebted to them for their persistent care and concern over the last four decades. Everyone should have such mentors and friends.

Introduction

When I was in high school, many decades ago, I decided to read through the Bible. I was already kind of a geek at sixteen. When I noticed contradictions or strange stories, I added them to a list of questions I kept in the back of my Bible. When I finished, I went to my pastor with my questions. He was not a cool, hipster pastor in shorts and a Hawaiian shirt. He was older than my parents, and a little intimidating. I plowed through my list of questions and he patiently answered them. He did not dumb down his answers or oversimplify or demonstrate the slightest bit of criticism. I do not remember his answers, but I remember that this was safe space. He respected and honored my curiosity and my intellect. He encouraged my effort to engage with the Bible and understand it.

In college I attended a fundamentalist church for a while. The pastor preached through Paul's First Letter to the Corinthians in excruciating detail, and I was intrigued. He proclaimed *the* definitive interpretation of the Bible. Meanwhile, I was studying religion in college and encouraged by my deeply Christian professors to explore the contradictions and complexities of Scripture along with the examples of divine grace. There were many days when I found it difficult to live in the tension between the two views of the Bible. The preacher had all the answers, which we were expected to agree with and obey. The professors created a safe space to explore the ambiguities of the Bible. This questioning focus eventually carried the day for me. I have spent almost three decades teaching and preaching about the Bible, the history of Christianity, and the role of women in religion and society.

Last summer I taught a course on women in the Old Testament to pastors who were working on an advanced degree in preaching. At the end of the week, they all preached sermons on some of the most violent and difficult texts in the Bible. Many of us were repeatedly in tears after hearing these creative and sensitive sermons that conveyed the beauty, pain, and vulnerability of the stories. As we evaluated the course, they thanked one another for creating a safe space where they could discuss the difficult stories and then try to preach about them. The feelings of trust and safety they built together enabled them to take risks and try new approaches in their sermons.

I hope that this book will provide safe space for people to read, think, learn, converse, and disagree. You may not agree with everything I say. If you are reading this in a Bible study group, you will not agree with everything that other people say. Those who are relatively new to the Bible may find that some of the stories are very odd. The customs and practices are radically different from ours. Those who have grown up with the Bible sometimes forget how strange it is to people who are just starting to read it. If you are reading this in a Bible study, I encourage you to ask your honest questions and be willing to listen to the questions of others. The Bible is not harmed, and God is not offended, by even the most difficult questions about the stories and ideas in it.

I tell my students that when another student says something that they don't understand or don't agree with, a helpful response is, "Say more about that?" Sharp disagreement or an angry response to a biblical story may mean that someone has been harmed by a misguided interpretation in the past. Or they think that the Bible has been misused to harm other people. I encourage readers to bring questions, disagreements, and irritations. The more you engage with the Bible, the more it will come alive for you.

As you read and think about the Bible, either alone or in a group, I hope that you see the grace of God in the Bible and in each other. I hope that you see and experience that you are God's beloved. You are enough. You are worthy. You have wisdom and insight and personal connections that you bring to your study of the Bible.

The Bible is a complicated book. The New Testament was written about two thousand years ago in a culture very different from ours. In the chapters that follow, I try to explain the various stories in their cultural context, as I would to my students when we study the Bible. Before we can understand what the Bible means for us now, we need to understand what it meant in its own time. How would a person in the first century have related to Jesus? Or worked alongside Paul in the early church?

We have often been taught to look at the Bible as a rule book, or as a collection of stories with morals that tell us how to live. Sometimes that is true, but the Bible is more than an instruction book for life, not least because it is often so difficult to live as the Bible teaches. The Bible is not a checklist of tasks we must accomplish to earn God's approval. Instead, the Bible is a story about the love that God and Jesus have for flawed human beings. In the New Testament, the focus is particularly on Jesus and how he related to people during his life on earth and continued to inspire them when he was no longer physically present.

The Bible may be two thousand years old, but it continues to help us to make sense of our lives. It is a mirror in which we see first-century people struggling with some of the same issues that we experience today: the power of human sin to hurt others and ourselves, the power of shame and guilt, and the power of grace and love to heal and to make new. In Scripture we see Jesus modeling courageous and healthy ways of living. We see human beings modeling selfish, greedy, and mean-spirited ways of living. We also see human beings who are transformed by the love of Jesus and the power of the Holy Spirit. We see grace. We see love. We see God.

In the chapters that follow, I include a number of details about the various stories. My students occasionally complain that I am "picking apart the text" in a way that is too detailed and critical for their liking. But my experience is that the more I learn about the Bible, the more I understand it, the more sense it makes, and the more relevant and interesting it becomes. The more I learn, the more I see that the Bible is incredibly complex.[1]

This book explores the women in the New Testament. It is a companion to my earlier book about women in the Old Testament.[2] This book was in some ways more challenging to write, because the New Testament stories about women do not provide much material to work with. The women often do not speak. They are not named. They do not do very much. In the Gospels, women are often present in the story to give Jesus an opportunity to heal or to say something profound. The text does not tell us what the women were thinking or feeling.

That leads to some imaginative speculation on the part of the writer and the readers. I am not making things up, exactly, but I am trying to put myself in the place of the women in these stories and consider what they might be thinking and feeling. At times I speculate about their motivations. I do not offer these as a definitive interpretation, and you may well disagree with the way I read the stories. I hope that you will see my efforts as a way to make each story come alive for you. I hope that you will find ways that the story resonates with your own experience. It's a different time, of course, but there are many places of connection.

Getting to Know the New Testament

The New Testament includes four Gospels, which are "according to" Matthew, Mark, Luke, and John. The first three are relatively similar and often tell similar stories. John is distinctive in style and quite different from the other three.

Mark is the earliest Gospel, probably written about 70 CE. Matthew and Luke probably were written around 80–90 CE, and John about 90–100 CE. The late dates of authorship mean that the Gospels were probably not written by the disciples with those names. In the first century, writing in someone else's name was seen as a compliment, not an act of plagiarism. In this book, I will refer to the authors as they have been commonly known.

The book of the Acts of the Apostles was part of a two-volume series along with the Gospel of Luke. The earliest books of the New Testament are the various letters of Paul to the churches. These were probably written in the 50s, about two decades after the ministry of Jesus.

The Gospels tell a story about the life, ministry, death, and resurrection of Jesus, but they are not simply recording facts. They are trying to reflect on the meaning of Jesus' life and death several decades after he lived and died. Most of the early Christians never met Jesus, but only heard about him. Many of them lived in an urban environment that was very different from Galilee, where Jesus lived. The Gospel writers wanted to say something meaningful to the early Christians about who this Jesus was and what they might learn from his life and death and resurrection. How might the teachings and actions help them understand what it meant to follow Jesus? How to make decisions? How to relate to other people?

It was particularly important to reflect on the meaning of the life and ministry of Jesus because the early Christians lived in a hostile environment. Jesus proclaimed a grace-filled new way to live that welcomed and included all people. Similarly, the apostle Paul proclaimed equality and respect for women, slaves, and the poor in the new Christian communities. This was the ideal for Christian communities, but they lived in a society that did not always permit such gracious and inclusive ways of life. First-century society was broken and damaged in many ways. Powerful, wealthy men ruled at the top. Slaves, women, and poor people served at the bottom. How do people live according to Christian values in a society whose values are opposed to the Christian faith? The early Christians did not agree about the answer to that question, and Christians have been debating it ever since.

It might have been easier if Jesus had led his people out to the desert to start a new Christian community unencumbered by the values of the world. He might have created a utopia where Christians could live just as Jesus told them to live, without being affected by the bad behavior of other human beings. It is worth noting that when groups of Christians have tried to do that in the past, the communities have lasted only a generation or so. It turns out that even Christian communities behave badly and eventually self-destruct.

Jesus did not try to build a safe, isolated community. Instead, he expected his disciples to build a Christian community in a culture that was not Christian. This would not be easy, and it would require constant conversation and negotiation. How do you live in a world that does not share your values and ideals? How do you live in a culture that enslaves people and demeans women, when the Christian faith advocates equality and respect for all? Do Christians modify their ideals of inclusion so as not to offend the Roman government? How do Christians present themselves when people outside their community do not understand their beliefs? These kinds of questions are relevant in many of the stories that follow.

Jesus and Women

The Bible contains far too many stories in which women are shamed, shunned, and generally treated badly. The events of the Bible occurred in a patriarchal culture where women were treated badly, and the people in the Bible reflected their culture. Men often behaved badly toward women, not because God told them to do so, but because their culture did.[3] The culture of the first century expected women to be wives and mothers who were quiet and submissive. They were not encouraged to learn or to lead. They lived in a shame-based culture where modesty and sexual propriety were the most important female values. Those who were not considered modest could be shunned and shamed.

Jesus did not do this. He treated women as fully human, not as sexual objects. One of the best descriptions of Jesus and women appears in an essay Dorothy Sayers wrote in 1947:

> Perhaps it is no wonder that the women were first at the Cradle and last at the Cross. They had never known a man like this Man— there never has been such another. A prophet and teacher who never nagged at them, never flattered or coaxed or patronized; who never made arch jokes about them, never treated them either as "The women, God help us!" or "The ladies, God bless them!"; who rebuked without querulousness and praised without condescension; who took their questions and arguments seriously; who never mapped out their sphere for them, never urged them to be feminine or jeered at them for being female; who had no axe to grind and no uneasy male dignity to defend; who took them as he found them and was completely unself-conscious. There is no act, no sermon, no parable in the whole Gospel that borrows its pungency from female perversity; nobody could possibly guess from the words and deeds of Jesus that there was anything "funny" about women's nature.[4]

This is the Jesus you will encounter in the stories that follow.

Jesus encouraged and supported women. When they were shamed or limited or restricted, he affirmed them and expanded their sphere of action. Jesus ministered in the first century, and yet Jesus continues to inspire support and encouragement for women. Melinda Gates has been motivated by her Christian faith and the life of Jesus to encourage and support women around the world. She writes, "When you lift up women, you lift up humanity. . . . How can we create a moment of lift in human hearts so that we all *want* to lift up women? Because sometimes all that's needed to lift women up is to stop pulling them down."[5]

Gates tells the story of Sister Sudha Varghese, who became a nun to serve the poorest of the untouchable Indians, the Musahar or "rat eaters." In 2005 she established a free boarding school for the Musahar girls. These girls had consistently been told that they were dirt. They were the last, the least. They deserved nothing and should expect nothing. The girls constantly looked down at the ground and refused to make eye contact. Varghese began a program in which the girls learned karate, and eventually they competed and did well at national and international competitions. When they went to other countries, they were treated with respect. They began to see that when they were treated badly in their own country it was not because of a flaw in them, but a defect in their society.

Gates observed that if a woman is loved and supported, she gains self-confidence, she sees her gifts and her power, and she defends her rights. "You lift their gaze," Gates says. "They gain their voice." When a woman changes her view of herself, she can start to change the culture that keeps her down. She will challenge the status quo. She will resist oppression.[6]

These strategies of affirmation, inclusion, and acceptance are particularly important, because many people hear just the opposite: a strong message that they are not worthy, not good enough, and they should be ashamed of themselves. This attitude is not confined to beliefs about untouchables in developing countries; it exists in all cultures.

Brené Brown is the guru of shame research and a brilliant speaker and writer.[7] She says that shame has two messages. First, you are not good enough, pretty enough, smart enough, strong enough, macho enough, etc. Second, if you can get beyond these judgments and find a place in the world, you will hear a voice saying, "Who do you think you are?" We begin to hear these voices early in our lives, whenever we turn on the television or open a magazine or visit a shopping mall. We hear these voices in school, in church, at work, and in our families.

Brown explains that guilt is a feeling that we have done something bad. Guilt can be useful, because when we do something wrong we can acknowledge it, apologize, and make better choices in the future. Shame, on the other hand, is the feeling that I *am* bad. Shame says that you are not worthy, you are not capable, you are broken and sinful and disgusting. Shame grows best in secrecy and silence, and the best antidote to shame is empathy, where someone else says, "Me too," and you realize you are not alone. Someone sees you and affirms you, and you might feel the shame begin to lift a bit.

Brown's work is relevant to a discussion of women in the New Testament because shame is a dominant theme in these stories. Mary feels shame for an early pregnancy. Elizabeth feels shame for being barren. The woman with the bleeding disease feels shame because she is unclean. The woman who is bent over feels shame for having a disease. And then there are the various "sinful" women who have multiple marriages or bad reputations. The culture shames these women, but Jesus does not. Jesus sees the women. He acknowledges and affirms them. He heals their bodies and their souls. And he never puts them down or calls them unworthy.

Late in the fourth century, the preacher John Chrysostom referred to the women mentioned in the book of Romans as "more spirited than lions."[8] It is a good description of many women in the New Testament. I hope that you enjoy learning about them.

1

The Birth of Jesus

MARY THE MOTHER OF JESUS
(Luke 1–2 and Others)

Mary the mother of Jesus may be the most revered woman in the world. She has inspired thousands of books and paintings. She is a central figure in nativity scenes and Christmas pageants. Churches are built and named in her honor. Devout Catholics pray to her daily. And yet, little is known about her. The Bible contains fewer than a hundred verses recording her words or actions.[1]

The Roman Catholic tradition portrays Mary as a powerful yet approachable figure who intercedes with her son Jesus on behalf of sinful humanity. She is someone to adore. She is supposed to be imitated, also, but she is an impossible ideal, since ordinary women cannot be both virgin and mother. Mary is a hard act to follow.

Many Protestant Christians are not sure how to relate to Mary. She might be the subject of a sermon at Christmas, but otherwise she is rarely mentioned. Some Protestants have viewed her as little more than a channel for the birth of Jesus. Her body and breasts sustained him in infancy, but she played only a minimal role in the rest of Jesus' life. Still, she was significant, and some Protestants have been increasingly drawn to Mary and want to know more about her.

Protestants usually start with the Bible, where the stories about Mary are minimal but reveal a woman of substance.

Mary Conceives (Luke 1)

Luke 1 begins with a story about another unusual birth. Zechariah, an elderly priest, receives a visit from the angel Gabriel, who announces that his elderly wife, Elizabeth, will bear a son. (See the following section on Elizabeth.)

A few months later, the angel appears again, this time to a woman named Mary. She was probably more girl than woman, perhaps as young as twelve or thirteen. She was engaged to a man named Joseph, but had not yet gone to live with him.

Mary lived in Nazareth, a small town of no significance. She was not wealthy or famous. She may not have been particularly spiritual, even though much of the artwork portraying the angel's visit shows Mary devoutly reading or praying in a holy beam of light. She was more likely cooking or cleaning or caring for a younger sibling. She was shocked to see an angel appear in the midst of her everyday life. The angel says, "Greetings, favored one! The Lord is with you." This perplexes her. She does not understand how she can be favored or why an angel is coming to her.

The angel explains that she has been graced by God, not because of her personal achievements or perfection,[2] but because God has chosen her for a task and given her the abilities to do it. She will conceive and bear a son. The child will not be ordinary but will be the Messiah, the Savior of the world. Again, she is puzzled. "How can this be, since I am a virgin?" She is not skeptical so much as curious about how this birth could happen outside the usual pattern.[3]

The angel responds that the Holy Spirit will come over her and the power of the Most High (God) will overshadow her.[4] God's presence with, around, and over her will make a miracle happen. In past stories, God's power has made old women (Sarah, Elizabeth) and infertile women (Rebekah, Rachel, Hannah) conceive, but Mary's son will be greater than all of them. God will accomplish the birth of Mary's son in an even more miraculous way—without a man!

In contrast to the way she is sometimes pictured, Mary is not passive or submissive here. She talks back and asks questions. She is willing to say yes to God even though she does not fully understand what she is in for. She is not merely a passive womb or food source for Jesus. God does not force her, or assume she will say yes, but takes her seriously as a partner in the process of giving birth to Jesus.

This is astounding news, but Mary will pay a price. Matthew reports in his Gospel that Joseph learned that Mary was pregnant and knew that he was not the father. Her apparent adultery was punishable by death, but Joseph decided to end the marriage without publicly humiliating her. An angel appeared and gave him the astounding news that the baby was from God and that Joseph should continue his relationship with Mary. Joseph took the angel's advice, but he must have been curious about these strange events.

Mary was in an awkward situation with her out-of-wedlock pregnancy. Who would believe her if she said the baby was from God? Perhaps as an escape, and perhaps seeking support from another woman in a similar situation, Mary traveled about ninety miles to see her older relative Elizabeth. Mary may have been anxious and uncertain. She may have felt ashamed, even though she had done nothing wrong, and she probably felt the usual exhaustion and hormonal upheaval of early pregnancy. She may have wondered whether Joseph would accept her, whether she would be ostracized by the community, and whether she would be a good enough mother to this child. Elizabeth probably had her own concerns about surviving her pregnancy and delivery, and providing adequate care for a baby at her age.

When Mary arrives at her home, Elizabeth feels her own unborn baby move, and she interprets this as a sign that her baby recognizes Mary's baby. Elizabeth discerns that Mary has been chosen for something important. Elizabeth announces that Mary and her child have been "blessed," which means spoken well of, and Elizabeth speaks these supportive words at a time when Mary may have desperately needed the assurance and affirmation. Elizabeth recognizes God's blessing of Mary, and says in essence, "You go, girl! You are special! And your baby is special!"

Perhaps the affirmation helps Mary to find her voice and her confidence, because she responds to Elizabeth with a stunning song (Luke 1:46–55). It is called the Magnificat because it begins, "My soul magnifies the Lord." It is not a sweet lullaby, but a song of praise to the God who is turning the world upside down. Mary sings that God has "looked with favor on the lowliness of [God's] servant." In the world's eyes, Mary is young, female, and poor, and yet God has chosen to do a radical new thing in her: to take on flesh and enter the world.

Mary's song announces an astounding reversal of fortunes. God will bring down the powerful from their thrones and lift up the lowly. The hungry will be filled, and the rich will be empty. In this moment, Mary feels the world's balance shift toward the poor and lowly, and away from the rich and powerful. Mary had already said yes to God, and here she says a resounding no to oppression!

Mary Gives Birth to Jesus (Luke 2)

The birth of Jesus happens in the usual way, as all human babies are born, so how was it special? Luke hints at something unusual when he reports the names of rulers and the demand for a census. He is suggesting that although the Roman Empire may think it has all the power in the world, this baby, born to an insignificant girl, will be even more powerful and will one day transform the world.

Mary and Joseph traveled to Bethlehem and probably found shelter in the home of relatives. Other relatives with more seniority may have claimed the guest room, so Mary and Joseph likely stayed in the animals' pen attached to the home.

Luke reports the birth of Jesus matter-of-factly. Mary gave birth to Jesus, "wrapped him in bands of cloth, and laid him in a manger." Nevertheless, the story is often romanticized. Imagine a Sunday school Christmas pageant where the ten-year-old girl playing Mary wears a blue robe, maybe with a basketball under her robe to simulate pregnancy. When the time comes for her to deliver the baby, she quickly removes the basketball and cradles a doll in her arms. Obviously the pageant is not going to include full-strength labor pains and bodily fluids, but no actual human birth happens this neatly and painlessly.

Mary has often been portrayed as completely calm and comfortable. The Cathedral of Chartres outside Paris contains the dress that Mary supposedly wore when she gave birth to Jesus. It is a length of beige silk without a single bloodstain. Did she really feel no discomfort, shed no blood, despite the reality of a large head proceeding through a narrow passageway?

When my students discuss the birth of Jesus, they read a little poem expressing the stark reality of childbirth using language of blood and pain and pushing. Some students find it crude and disturbing to hear that Mary pushed Jesus out between sticky thighs. They prefer to think that Mary looked like Princess Kate, who was photographed outside the hospital mere hours after giving birth, wearing a designer dress and stilettos, with perfect hair and makeup.

A photo of the Holy Family taken several hours after the birth of

Jesus might more realistically have shown an exhausted Mary, still sore from the birth, struggling to help the baby latch on and begin to nurse. Other family members may have been in and out of the room, even as the new parents longed for sleep and privacy. Baby Jesus may have been more irritable and fussy than meek and mild. Like all babies, he cried when he was hungry or irritable or wet or lonely, because that is how babies communicate. Like all babies, he was vulnerable and dependent and would survive only with the care of loving and patient parents.

Why dwell on the gritty details? Because a realistic picture of the birth of Jesus makes the incarnation even more powerful. God did not take on indestructible human flesh. Jesus was not a bionic baby, born to a woman who felt nothing but bliss. Contrary to the lyrics of "Away in a Manger," which claim that Jesus did not cry, the point of the incarnation is that Jesus became like us, in all our weakness and in all our humanity.

Mary was also a profoundly ordinary mother, and she probably had many questions. Would she be able to feed this child? Could she keep him safe? Would she love him? The Holy Spirit did not provide a Dr. Spock manual of child care. Mary and Joseph had to figure out the parenting process by trial and error, as all parents do.

If the birth of Jesus was relatively ordinary, the arrival of the shepherds was not. Imagine Mary's surprise when strange men appeared at the door telling of angels who proclaimed this baby Savior and Messiah. After the shepherds had come and gone, Mary "treasured all these words and pondered them in her heart" (Luke 2:19). This, too, is often sentimentalized, as if Mary were making a baby book, but she was wrestling with the meaning of these unusual events. She may have been wondering what she and Joseph had gotten themselves into.

Mary's ongoing role in the life of Jesus is often minimized, as if she were irrelevant once Jesus emerged from her womb. But Jesus needs his mother: her milk, her love, her lap, her gaze, and her wisdom. She will raise this child. She will teach him to be a good Jewish boy, to love and keep the Law, and to know God. She and Joseph will help Jesus grow into a man of wisdom and integrity.

In Luke's final scene of the infant Jesus (2:22–38), Mary and Joseph take Jesus to the temple. They are again reminded that this is no ordinary child when an elderly priest named Simeon announces that God is bringing salvation to the world through this baby. About the same time, an elderly woman named Anna recognizes that the baby Jesus is the source of redemption she and her people had been waiting for. (See the next section for more on Anna.) What would a young woman of thirteen think of this lofty talk about her infant?

Mary as Mother of Jesus as a Young Man and Adult

The family returned home to Nazareth, and Luke reports that the child grew and became strong and wise. He includes one scene of Jesus at age twelve, the only glimpse we have of his childhood. Mary and Joseph and Jesus have gone to Jerusalem to worship at the temple. On the way home, the couple realize that Jesus is not with any of their extended family. Mary panics, as every mother would. When she finally finds him in the temple, three days later, she is a little annoyed. She might have asked, "Why did you do this? Didn't you realize we would be terrified?" Jesus gives her a bit of a brush-off in response. "Did you not know that I must be in my Father's house?" (2:49). We can imagine her saying, "Well, maybe so, but right now you are twelve and you need to tell us where you are!" Mary was the mother of an extraordinary child, but that does not mean they avoided the usual issues of adolescence.

Once Jesus becomes an adult and enters into public ministry, the Gospels rarely mention Mary, and yet she seems to be present in his life. Mark writes that Jesus' mother and siblings[5] once tried to remove him from a volatile situation because some people thought he was out of his mind (Mark 3:21). Mary is often criticized for this apparent lack of faith in and support for her son, but she must have been terrified. She would surely have known that the challenge Jesus posed to the Jewish religious leaders would not end well. Perhaps she hoped that if she could get him to come home and be quiet she could save him from an early death.

In the Gospel of John, Mary appears at a wedding along with Jesus and the disciples. The wine runs out before the party is over. Mary notices and informs Jesus, who seems to dismiss her as a helicopter parent. "Woman, what concern is that to you and to me? My hour has not yet come" (John 2:1–4). She is not put off by his tone and tells the servants to do what Jesus says. She is significant in the story because she recognizes the power Jesus possesses and encourages him to use it. Perhaps he was hesitant and needed a motherly push. She also encourages other people to obey him. She is a witness to Jesus like Mary and Martha and the Samaritan woman.

Mary at the Crucifixion and After

Mary appears in John's Gospel at the crucifixion of Jesus. She stands at the foot of the cross with "the disciple whom he [Jesus] loved" (John 19:25–27), and in one of his last statements before dying, Jesus commends Mary and the disciple to each other. They were to build a new family, based not on biology but on love for Jesus. This kind of relationship would form the heart of the early church.

In one final mention, Mary appears in Acts 1:14 as one of a group of disciples who gather after the ascension of Jesus. That is all that the Bible says about her. We are left with a lot of unanswered questions.

Christian women have often been taught to imitate Mary's obedience and submission, but Mary is neither spineless nor mindlessly obedient. She is not forced to bear Jesus, but says an active yes to God even though she does not fully understand what she is in for. In that she is a model of faith which has only enough light to see the next step. She is not a porcelain princess or a saintly superhero. She is a real woman who experiences deep grief and loss and joy.

Diving Deeper

Favored one. Can ordinary people be graced or favored in the way that Mary was? What if an angel came to you and said, "Greetings, favored one! The Lord is with you"? Would you respond with a sarcastic "Yeah, right"? Would you look behind you for the person the angel really meant? Would you say, "No, not me. I'm not spiritual enough"?

So many voices tell people they are not good enough. Children and teens are mocked for their appearance or sexual identity or choices in clothing. Adults constantly hear via advertising that they are not attractive enough, fit enough, thin enough, successful enough. Maybe we have heard disapproval from our parents or the church or our teachers. What a contrast to hear that we have been graced by God. We are affirmed. We are enough.

Here is the wonderful paradox of the good news. No one is good enough, and yet God's grace and favor come to us. Grace comes not because we've earned it, but because God chooses to be gracious, to call us and equip us for tasks. Not the task of bearing Jesus. That's been done. But tasks that help the world become a place where peace and goodwill become more of a reality.

Handmaid of the Lord. Mary is sometimes portrayed as an obedient, subservient handmaid who meekly accepted the role God prepared for her. This is not a particularly inviting image for contemporary women who are increasingly trying to say no, set boundaries, and lean in. After millennia of serving and caring, women are reevaluating those roles and sometimes refusing to automatically perform those tasks. Men are also reevaluating their roles and sometimes deciding that they need to do *more* serving and caring, especially for their children. The image of being a slave, even if softened to "handmaid," is not very helpful. Women have too often been told to give up their career aspirations in order to care for a husband and children. If they do work outside the home, they are still expected to fulfill all the obligations of a good wife and mother.

Rather than see Mary as an obedient slave, we might see her as a disciple. She trusted God enough to say yes to the first step, even though she could not anticipate everything that would happen in the future. She could say yes to God while having fears and questions.

Ideal woman? Is Mary a role model for contemporary women? In what ways? If we see Mary as more like us, can we become more like Mary? What might it mean for a person today to freely and joyfully say yes to the invitation to participate in God's work in the world?

Blessed. Being blessed here means that God or someone else is saying, "Well done." It's an affirmation. Not just for what Mary does, but also for who she is. It is God saying, "You are loved, you are worthy, you are valuable, you are enough." To feel blessed is the opposite of feeling shamed, discouraged, worthless, and isolated.

Good news to the poor. The song of Mary has been a powerful source of encouragement to people who are poor and oppressed because it seems to say that God is on their side. During the civil war in Guatemala (1960–1996) between a repressive government and people who were seeking basic human rights and economic opportunity, many people quoted the Magnificat to support their conviction that God was on the side of the poor and would overthrow the powerful. It empowered the poor in a way that frightened the rich and powerful.

Questions for Reflection and Discussion

What does it mean to be favored? Does God look with favor upon other people than Mary?

How do you see Mary? Is she a porcelain princess? A prim-faced saint with a halo? Is she holy? In what way? How is she a role model to contemporary women?

What do you think about the explicit language about childbirth in this chapter? Are you offended? Why?

How much did Mary comprehend about the identity of Jesus? How was he a divine being and yet a human child and teenager at the same time?

How does Mary's song speak today to those who are poor and oppressed? To those who are privileged?

ELIZABETH AND ANNA
(Luke 1–2)

One of the great joys of my life has been opportunities for friendship with women who are a generation older than I am. I first met Jetts at church when I was in my late twenties and she was in her seventies. I had a young son and was juggling being a mother and writing my dissertation. She had four children and had retired from a long teaching career. She and her husband had an egalitarian marriage. He cooked and she baked pies. They each paid half the household expenses out of their own checking accounts. Jetts was brilliant, passionate, elegant, funny, and a joy to be with. She had been a feminist before I was born. I learned so much from her, and I still miss her.

Women of a certain age can be a great gift. They are often a source of wisdom and insight. They often do not care what anyone thinks of them anymore, so they can be extra bold and courageous. Unfortunately, they are not always respected and valued. My friend Elizabeth complains that when men have white hair they are seen as wise and distinguished, but when women have white hair they are seen as old.

In the stories of Elizabeth and Anna, we discover two women who play a role in the birth of Jesus. They are in the second half of their lives. They have not achieved greatness. They are not famous. They have spent their lives waiting for something to happen. Elizabeth waited to have a baby. Anna waited to see a promised baby. Their stories remind us that women of a certain age also have stories to tell, and that people of all ages can be vehicles for God's Spirit.

Elizabeth

Elizabeth was married to Zechariah, who served as a priest for the Israelite people. The author of the Gospel reports that both of them were righteous and blameless before God. They were good people who obeyed all the commandments, but they had no children, and they were old. The author reports that Elizabeth was barren. (Childlessness was almost always assumed to be the woman's "fault.") The Greek word for barren is *steiros*, which relates to the English word "sterile." It suggests that her womb was hard or stiff and incompatible with new life. Infertility was usually considered a divine judgment for bad behavior, but that is not the case here. Elizabeth and Zechariah are righteous, but that was no consolation for the lack of children.

Elizabeth would have felt both personal pain and social stigma over this. Bearing children, especially sons, was a woman's primary role and purpose in life. If she had no children, she was nothing but a failure. She brought suffering and shame on her husband. Her future was at risk, because she would have no one to care for her after her husband died, and she would die alone. She may have felt shamed and disgraced, but that was not the end of the story. Their lack of a child was not a punishment but an occasion for God to act.

Zechariah was taking his turn as a priest serving in the temple when an angel appeared to him. Zechariah was terrified, because even priests do not expect to see divine messengers appear in their workplace. The angel told Zechariah that he and Elizabeth would have a son, but Zechariah was skeptical and wanted some proof. "How will I know that this is so?" He thought that conception was physically impossible. "I am old," he said. "I am Gabriel," the angel responded.[6] Human impossibility meets divine possibility. Human limitation meets divine activity.

These unusual births occurred several times in the Old Testament. Sarah, Rebekah, Rachel, Hannah, and the mother of Samson all struggled with infertility. Each time God intervened to take away what they saw as their disgrace. Each woman gave birth to a special boy (Isaac, Jacob, Joseph, Samuel, and Samson) who was destined to play a significant role in Israel's history. Elizabeth was another woman in this group.

Angel messengers are usually fairly tolerant of the shock they provoke by their appearance, but Gabriel thought that Zechariah was overly skeptical. Not only did Zechariah not believe the angel, but he asked for proof of the promise, and as a result, the angel announced that Zechariah would be unable to speak until the baby was born! He may have lost his hearing also, since people later wrote notes to him. How did he communicate this profound experience to Elizabeth, since she may not have been able to read? The text does not say, but they did not need words to conceive a child!

Elizabeth was delighted! After all those years of shame and self-doubt, she was finally going to have a baby! She was grateful to God, who had seen her and taken away her disgrace. She may have felt the wild mix of emotions common to pregnancy: elation, relief, anxiety, and fear. She hid herself at home for five months. The whole experience may have felt too good to be true. Perhaps she wanted to enjoy the pregnancy herself without nosy neighbors who were shocked that someone so old was pregnant.

When Elizabeth was six months pregnant, the angel Gabriel made another visit, this time to a young woman named Mary. (See previous section.) Gabriel announced that Mary would conceive, before she was officially married to her husband. Pregnant too early, Mary may have wanted to avoid potential suspicion and criticism from her community, so she traveled ninety miles to visit her relative Elizabeth. Ninety miles was not a two-hour road trip but a six-day walk. Elizabeth must have been a significant person in Mary's life for her to have traveled so far. Elizabeth offered the possibility of safe space and companionship to Mary, who was probably only about thirteen at the time.

When Mary entered Elizabeth's house and greeted her, Elizabeth's baby "leaped in her womb" (Luke 1:41). Her body and baby recognized the baby in Mary's body, even before Mary told Elizabeth the news. So here are two pregnant women together, one having a baby late in life, and the other having a baby when she was very young and unmarried.

Elizabeth was a wise and compassionate friend, but she was more than that. Elizabeth was filled with the Holy Spirit, and she was a prophet. She discerned that Mary was pregnant with an extraordinary baby. Others might have criticized and shamed Mary for being pregnant before marriage, but Elizabeth saw God at work. Elizabeth was so filled with joy that she could not help but affirm Mary. "Blessed are you among women, and blessed is the fruit of your womb" (1:42). She saw that God had chosen and graced Mary. Something special was happening, and Elizabeth was amazed that she was fortunate enough to be participating in the process. "Why has this happened to me, that the mother of my Lord comes to me?" (v. 43). Elizabeth was the first person to acknowledge that the baby Mary was carrying was not ordinary. Mary was the mother of her Lord! This baby would be the Savior or Messiah whom Elizabeth and the Israelites had been waiting for.

Two women. Bodies changing and expanding, sometimes in uncomfortable ways. Two women. Elizabeth with her shame taken away by pregnancy. Mary with a shame caused by her pregnancy. Two women, both about to become mothers of special boys.

There are very few stories in the Bible where two women are together without competition and arguments. This story is an example of solidarity between women who want to be together. They are friends who support and bless each other. Elizabeth provided affirmation, acceptance, and safe space, but she also helped Mary find her voice. Back home in Nazareth, Mary may have worried about propriety. What would people think? What would they say? She may have been eager to get away from the prying and the counting and the tut-tutting. The pregnancy may have felt like more of a burden than a blessing. But in this safe space with Elizabeth, Mary may have been able to experience joy and delight. God had chosen her! How amazing was that? In the presence of someone who loved and accepted her, Mary poured out her song that we know as the Magnificat. Mary sang of God who will transform the world! Bring down the powerful. Raise up the lowly. Turn the world upside down. In this space together, the two of them realized that their pregnancies were not just for their delight. Their children were signs that God was doing a new thing in the world.

When Elizabeth gave birth to her son, her neighbors and relatives saw the baby as a sign of God's mercy, and they rejoiced with her. On the eighth day, when it was time to circumcise the baby, the relatives assumed he would be named Zechariah, after his father. Elizabeth said, "No; he is to be called John" (Luke 1:60). They did not believe her, so they motioned to Zechariah to get his input. He cast the decisive vote when he wrote that the baby's name was John. Finally, Zechariah got his voice back. He sang his own joyful song about how baby John would be a prophet who would prepare the way and show the world the ways of God.

Before he could live out his vocation as a prophet, John had to grow up. The mothers of children, even the special boys, do not simply give birth and then become irrelevant. Zechariah and Elizabeth helped the boy John to learn, experience life, and become strong in spirit. They prepared him for the difficult life that awaited him.

Anna

Anna was a strong, independent older woman who is recognized for her wisdom, insight, and persistence. She was either eighty-four years old or had been a widow for eighty-four years, which would make her almost a hundred years old. She, along with the elderly Simeon, had spent most of their long lives in the temple waiting for the Messiah, the one who would redeem and restore Israel. She was a prophet, a term not often applied to women. She knew the teachings of Judaism. She knew redemption was coming, but she did not know when or how. Decades passed with no sign of the Messiah, but she came to the temple every day, waiting and watching, looking and listening. How many babies did she scrutinize? How many times did she ask if this baby was the one? Each time the answer was no. It was a fine baby, but it was not the Messiah. But she kept coming to the temple. She kept praying and hoping.

Mary and Joseph brought Jesus to the temple to carry out the required religious rituals. The prophet Anna also appeared in the temple, at just the right time. She saw Jesus and knew that he was the Messiah. She praised God, but the words of her song and teaching are not recorded. Luke does say that she told everyone in the room about the child Jesus and how he would someday redeem Jerusalem. How did she know Jesus was the one? Luke does not say.

Anna knew the history and tradition of her people. She kept alive the memory that God had promised a messiah. She told the story even when others forgot. Perhaps people grew a little irritated with the old woman who kept telling the old stories. But for her, the history and tradition were alive. She knew God would act, and she hoped she would live long enough to see it. She was a model of faith, piety, persistence, trust, and hope. She showed up every day, when it would have been easy to ease into retirement. She showed up every day, even though she must have grown discouraged. She showed up every day, even if she wondered whether she and the rest of the Jews had been completely wrong about waiting for the Messiah. She showed up every day, and finally Jesus showed up too.

Diving Deeper

Barren. Women may still feel disgraced if they are unable to conceive or carry a child to term. They may think they are being punished by God. They may experience a lot of grief if their bodies do not function as they hope. There are many social pressures, from would-be grandparents and from many other well-meaning people who wonder when the babies are coming. There is social stigma that suggests that a childless woman is incomplete.

The church sometimes contributes to the pressure on women to have children. At times churches have suggested or taught that childbearing is a woman's main role in life.

What about women who choose not to have children? Are they accepted? Or criticized for their choice? What about women who are labeled "barren" or "sterile"? They may pray for a miracle but still do not have children. How do childless women feel in your congregation? Do the church's expectations and assumptions contribute to their pain? Or does the church convey support and encouragement for the choices women make in their lives? And support and encouragement for those who are struggling with grief and loss?

Friends. The relationship between Elizabeth and Mary is a powerful example of female friendship that is rare in Scripture. It is also an example of intergenerational friendship. How do women of different ages support each other? How do they learn from each other? Parenting, for example, is hard work. It is often a thankless job that invites plenty of criticism. It can be helpful to hear from someone who has gone through the process and can assure younger parents that they are likely not doing irreparable harm to their children.

There are many other kinds of informal mentoring and support. How have our older friends managed work-life balance? A cancer diagnosis? A divorce? A spiritual crisis? The loss of a parent or child or spouse? How have they persisted and resisted throughout their lives?

Meanwhile, our younger friends provide valuable cultural knowledge. My students often fill me in on the latest cultural trends I know nothing about. They ask questions and offer insights that I have never considered. They offer energy, humor, insight, and deep wisdom of their own.

It is a gift to receive wisdom and insight from another person. It is also a gift to be perceived as a source of wisdom! It is a gift to be valued and heard and taken seriously. Everyone benefits from cross-generational friendships. Could you find someone older or younger than you, at work, in church, in a community organization, and invite them to coffee?

Wisdom. Anna is also a model of wisdom. She understood the past and looked forward to the future. Sometimes we dismiss older people as hopelessly outdated and irrelevant. We assume that whatever they know from the past is no longer relevant because the present is so radically different.

In interviews with retired ministers, I have always been struck by their wisdom about the church. Even though the church has changed dramatically during the last seventy years, some aspects of being an effective pastor do not change. My friend Carl was a pastor during the Vietnam War. Carl's mentor told him that he should always give people the space to talk, and listen carefully without trying to instruct or correct them. Then they might listen to the pastor.

Listen to people, be present for them, love them, even when it is hard. That is wise advice not only for pastors, but for all of us.

Alice Walker, in her novel *The Temple of My Familiar,* says that when an elder dies, it is as if a library is burned down. She gives these words to a woman who has studied the ways of the elders in her African community: "One thing I know . . . learning from one's elders does not permit pessimism. Your day is always easier than theirs. You look at them, so beautiful and so wise, and you cannot help trying to emulate them. It is courage given by osmosis, I think."[7]

Showing up every day. Like Anna, many of us wait a long time to see results. For a parent, a pastor, a teacher, an activist, a politician, and people in many other vocations and situations, there is not always much instant gratification. Some of the most rewarding words I hear come from the student who says, "I took your class ten years ago. I didn't realize it then, but your class made a difference in my life." Like Anna, we keep showing up every day, trusting that God is at work in our work, even if we do not always see the results.

Questions for Reflection and Discussion

Think about the people who have played an important role in your life. How have they supported and encouraged you? Do you have friends of other generations? How have you learned from older women? How have you been a friend, role model, or encourager to other women, particularly those younger than you? How have you been mentored? How have you mentored others?

When have you had to show up every day? What were you waiting for? What helped you keep going?

What do you want your retirement years to look like?

Where have you seen the wisdom of the elders?

2

The Healed

THE BOLD BLEEDING WOMAN
(Mark 5:21–43)

Two women need healing.* One is twelve years old, at the transition from childhood to womanhood. She is sick and near death. The other woman has had a bleeding disorder for twelve years. Two women. One twelve years old. One twelve years ill. They both meet Jesus.

The young girl is not named in the story. Her father was Jairus, the leader of a synagogue, which meant he had some power and influence in the community. Jairus saw that Jesus had the power to heal, so when his twelve-year-old daughter was near death, he came to Jesus and begged him to heal her. Jairus had the privilege of being male and a leader, and it was perfectly legitimate for him to come face-to-face with Jesus and ask for help. Jesus agreed to travel to Jairus's home.

On the way, they were interrupted by a desperate woman who had been ill with a bleeding disorder for twelve years. The literal translation of the Greek word is that she was "in a flux of blood," which sounds awkward and messy. She had spent all her money in search of medical help, but nothing had healed her. Most commentators assume that her disease was menstrual blood that never stopped, as this would be the most obvious source of bleeding in women. Such unexplained,

* The bleeding woman's story is also told in Matt. 9:18–26; Luke 8:40–56.

uncontrolled bleeding would have made her ritually unclean (Lev. 15:19–30). Anyone who touched her or sat on her bed became unclean also. Her condition may have ruined her marriage, if she married at all. She was probably isolated and lonely, because she was unwelcome in the traditional places of community, such as the synagogue and people's homes. The shame of the disease probably caused her and others to wonder what she had done to deserve such suffering.

My students always wonder why menstrual bleeding was considered unclean. Why were women ostracized and shamed for a natural process that leads to the desirable result of having children?

The rules in Leviticus 15 state that a woman was unclean for the seven days of her period and seven days after. Sexual contact was discouraged during this time. At the end of fourteen days, just when she could have sex with her husband without making him unclean, she was at the peak of her fertility.[1] The rules seem designed in part to maximize the chance for pregnancy.

At the end of the fourteen days, women had to offer two birds as a sacrifice to "make atonement on her behalf before the LORD for her unclean discharge" (Lev. 15:30). These rules were still in place for Jewish women in the first century. This need for sacrifice reinforces the belief that menstrual bleeding requires repentance because it is sinful, disgusting, and shameful.

It is possible that the rules existed not so much because menstruation was gross and disgusting but because it was mysterious and powerful. The process of pregnancy and childbirth was feared, respected, and poorly understood. The ability to bleed and not die was particularly strange, in a "wow, that's amazing" way more than an "ooh, that's disgusting" way. Women were thought to be connected to a powerful life-giving force, and the strict rules may have been an attempt to recognize the holiness and mystery of this life-giving process.

A monthly period is a sign of the power to create life, but its presence also signifies the absence of new life. A period means a woman is not pregnant, and in a culture where a woman's primary role was to bear children, a period signaled that she had "failed" that month. Perhaps the fourteen days of uncleanness gave space for a time of grieving.

This biological information helps to set the context for this story. If periodic monthly bleeding was bad, then constant bleeding was even worse. She was perpetually unclean. Whatever the religious intent of the rules might have been, in practice, they were a source of pain and grief for this woman. Her body did not work correctly, through no fault of her own. She was probably exhausted and anemic from the blood loss. She had spent all her money trying to get better, but nothing worked. And in addition to all this, the rules made her a social outcast.

She had multiple strikes against her. It was inappropriate for a woman to approach a man, but she had no father, husband, brother, or son who offered to approach Jesus on her behalf. She did not have the privilege of asking directly for what she needed, as Jairus did. And because of her illness, if she touched Jesus, or he touched her, he would have been made unclean as well, though only for a day. She did not think she was worthy to approach Jesus face-to-face. Years of shunning had taught her that.

So when she noticed Jesus moving in a crowd of people, she saw an opportunity. She would approach him from behind, quickly reach out to touch his coat, and then disappear into the crowd. It was the perfect strategy. Just as she expected, when she touched the edge of his clothes, she felt something change in her body, and she knew she was healed.

Her plan worked, except that Jesus also felt something! He knew that power had gone out of him and he asked, with more curiosity than anger, who had touched him. The disciples pointed out that crowds of people were pushing at him, but Jesus knew the touch was not accidental but deliberate. Finally, though she was tempted to flee, the woman fell down before him "in fear and trembling" and told him the whole truth. She knew he might be angry about her audacity. She told him about the long years of illness that had weakened and impoverished her. She described her confidence that Jesus could heal her if she touched him. Jesus listened without shaming or chastising her.

She did not think she was worthy of a face-to-face encounter, but Jesus did. He listened. He acknowledged her faith and personhood. He called her "Daughter," which gave her a new sense of identity. Once healed, she could reenter the religious community as a member of the family. Salvation for her was not simply fixing her malfunctioning body but also restoring her sense of well-being and connection.[2] She was made whole. Touching Jesus healed her body. Talking to Jesus healed her soul.

This was great news for her, but while Jesus and the woman engaged in meaningful conversation, Jairus was probably growing increasingly irritable and impatient. Surely his daughter who was dying *now* should have priority over this woman who had been sick for twelve years! Then the servants arrived with the devastating news that his daughter had died while he was on this fool's errand to save her. The servants pointed out that Jesus no longer needed to come, since the girl was already dead, but Jesus did not hesitate. He told Jairus not to be afraid (the same Greek word was used to describe the woman's fear) but to have faith (the same faith that made the woman well). This woman may have been an inconvenient interruption, but she was also a role model of how to trust in the power of Jesus. Her faith was exemplary.

Jesus arrived at Jairus's home and announced that the girl was not dead but sleeping. The crowd laughed. Jesus ignored the skeptics, entered the girl's room, took her by the hand, and said, "Little girl, get up," in Aramaic. She got up and walked around, and Jesus asked that she be given food, perhaps as proof that she was alive. He was willing to touch her, even though touching a dead body was taboo. Once again the possibility of ritual impurity did not bother Jesus. He did not recoil from touching a dead body or a diseased woman. The purity laws and taboos were less important to him than the value of healing through touch.

The young girl was a passive recipient of healing. She showed no faith at all, but her father trusted Jesus on her behalf. Jairus was still fearful, and his faith was not perfect, but it did not need to be. The power of God, and the words and touch of Jesus, brought about the girl's healing. She was a daughter in a loving family, and she needed to be brought to life and back into the embrace of the family who thought they had lost her.

The woman was also fearful, but her faith compelled her to reach out to Jesus, who saved her. She did not perform a magic mantra that earned her divine approval. The power of God, and the words and touch of Jesus, brought her to wholeness. Jesus called her a daughter and brought her back into the family of faith that had excluded her.

Diving Deeper

Initiative. The woman may have felt ashamed and unworthy of Jesus' attention, but she decided not to remain a victim. She took action. She made a plan and reached out for what she needed, but she did it indirectly. Rather than meet Jesus face-to-face, she came from behind and touched his clothes. When people feel ashamed and unworthy, they may find it difficult to ask for help. They may not have the energy for a grand gesture, like the women who anointed Jesus. But they may still find a way to say what they need or ask for something small. As in this woman's story, small steps of initiative and faith can work in tandem with God's healing power.

Sometimes it is strategic to take an indirect route to healing and transformation. Rosa Parks was not a preacher like Martin Luther King

Jr., but she was an activist. She refused to move to the back of the bus, and that sparked the Montgomery bus boycott, which ignited the civil rights movement of the 1950s and 1960s. Parks did not stay seated simply because she was tired. She was angry, and she chose to act in a way that challenged the Jim Crow segregation laws on the buses.[3]

Sometimes relatively small gestures can lead to significant change. Educational systems in some countries leave a lot to be desired, especially for girls. Overhauling the entire system in a particular area would require a great deal of time, energy, and knowledge. But there is one relatively low-cost way to improve education for girls. If they have access to sanitary products, they will not need to stay at home when they have their periods. Small businesses that make sanitary products have a double function of providing employment and keeping girls in school.

Some countries also experience high maternal mortality rates, but they are not necessarily best served by building expensive hospitals full of equipment. The attention of a midwife, the use of clean instruments to cut the umbilical cord, a prompt start to breast-feeding, and keeping the baby warm are relatively small actions that dramatically reduce the deaths of mother and child.[4]

Unclean. Jesus was not offended by people with diseases or frightened by the possibility of being made unclean. Instead, his healing power overcame the threat of contamination. In the late 1980s, when the means of transmission of HIV/AIDS was still not well known, many people avoided touching AIDS patients for fear of catching the disease. Princess Diana visited people with AIDS and chose not to wear a gown, mask, or gloves. She was photographed shaking the hand of a man with AIDS. She showed compassion without fear of contamination.

Touch is essential to human life and well-being. Jesus did not just tell the little girl to get up, but he took her hand. There can be serious problems with bad touching, but that should not make us so fearful and paralyzed that we forget the need for good touch. In health care, in church life, and in education, a safe, appropriate touch can be the vehicle for compassion, caring, and acceptance. Some elementary school teachers greet their students every day with a hug, a high five, a fist bump, or a dance. The students get to choose. Imagine the power of being greeted so warmly every day when you enter the classroom.

Daughter. The woman was alone, but Jesus welcomed her into a family. How have you felt welcomed and included? Have you ever been named specifically as a daughter? Carter Heyward was one of the first women to be ordained as an Episcopal priest. She received a letter from a woman who participated in a Communion service Heyward led soon after her ordination. The woman wrote: "I was unaware of the ways that I have felt excluded from God's inner circle of love until I experienced being included—both by the obvious fact of your inclusion and by you, as God's representative, including me. Somehow I feel I've spent my life trying to be God's son, only to realize at last that I am God's daughter."[5] Being included and welcomed is a powerful source of healing.

What if there is no happy ending? These two stories end well, with healing for both the girl and the woman. But we all know stories of people who pray and demonstrate deep faith, and are not healed. Does this mean their faith was weak? Or that they did not deserve healing? One of the great mysteries of faith and life is that "bad" people sometimes are rewarded or blessed, while "good" people suffer. Prayers are not always answered with healing. These are important questions and there is no shame in asking them.

These two stories do not answer our questions, but they do suggest that there is not necessarily a link between behavior or faith and life events. Bad things happen to good people, and good things happen to bad people. Jairus's position as a religious leader did not protect his family from hardship. Disease was not a punishment for bad behavior, and healing was not a reward for faith. Sickness is an unfortunate reality in a broken world. Healing is a sign of divine power and desire for wholeness and well-being. The reasons why some are healed and others are not are far above our pay grade. But God is present in all of it, to comfort, console, and encourage.[6]

Questions for Reflection and Discussion

This woman took a risk and defied social norms of her time. What risks have you taken? Not taken? What happened?

Can you think of examples of taking indirect action?

When have you felt included, welcomed as part of a family? Called a daughter? How have you welcomed others?

What has healing meant to you? Not just from a disease, but in the broadest sense of being made whole?

How might the meaning of this story be affected by the social distancing rules being practiced in the time of the COVID virus?

THE BENT-OVER WOMAN
(Luke 13:10–17)

Imagine that you have a disease that keeps you permanently bent over and unable to stand up straight. What do you see as you go about in the world? Can you see faces? Can you look people in the eye? No. Ordinarily as you go about your day you see feet, dirt, and trash.

The woman in this story was severely limited by her disease. She was bound by it, as if the disease had tied ropes and knots around her, limited her movements, and constricted her social interactions. She was an object of pity, curiosity, fear, and resentment.

Women throughout the world have been bound in various ways that have restricted their activity or limited their social contact. In China during the last millennium, many upper-class women had their feet bound tightly from birth, because tiny, misshapen feet were considered delicate and beautiful, even though women could not walk on them. Bound feet signified that a women was wealthy and could not be expected to perform field work or household chores.

Women in some African and Middle Eastern cultures are bound by the practice of female genital cutting. Long before they can consent, young girls, toddlers, and even babies undergo crude "surgery" that removes parts of their genitalia so they will not experience ordinary sexual pleasure. This practice is intended to keep them pure and faithful to their husbands, but it causes numerous physical problems. If a family refuses to impose this on their daughter, she may not be able to find a husband because she is considered dirty, shameful, and impure.

Some women are bound by a lack of birth control and by the expectation that women will happily give birth to ten or more children. Others are bound by the failure of their bodies to become pregnant or maintain a pregnancy to term. They may be bent over by the weight of infertility and miscarriage.[7]

Some people are bound by chronic diseases such as lupus, chronic fatigue syndrome, Crohn's, and other autoimmune diseases that are difficult to diagnose. They can feel miserable for several years while being told that the pain is all in their head. Others are bound by learning disabilities or depression or mental illness.

People can feel bound by social expectations. Women are supposed to be perfect mothers who don't permit junk food or too much screen time and are also high achievers at work. Men can also feel bound by social rules, particularly the expectation that men will never, ever be perceived as weak. The culture often teaches a kind of toxic masculinity which says that men must be tough and aggressive and in charge at all times.[8]

Finally, people in all parts of the world can be bound by poverty, lack of voice and vote in the political process, lack of jobs that pay a living wage, and sometimes a lack of basic personhood due to race or class or gender identity or sexual orientation.

Contemporary readers can identify with the woman in the story. We know what it means to feel bent over by the weight of expectations. There are so many ways to be bound.

In this story in Luke, Jesus was teaching in a synagogue on the Sabbath when a woman entered. She was crippled with a bone disease (what we call a dowager's hump, but worse), and she may have been shunned by religious people because her eighteen-year illness was thought to be a sign that God had punished her or that she was possessed by an evil spirit. Physical deformities were thought to be contagious, so it was best that "those people" stay inside their homes and not make other people uncomfortable. The people in the synagogue listening to Jesus may have tried not to look at her. Maybe they felt disgust for her. Maybe they were angry that she didn't just stay in her home. Maybe they wondered what she had done to deserve such a punishment. They saw her disability, but they did not see her.

Jesus saw her. He saw that she could not look anyone in the eye. He saw her pain. He saw her broken body, but he did not stare or pity or shame her. He called her over to him, touched her, and announced that she was set free or loosed from her ailment. The Greek word for "loosed" is the same word used to describe untying animals. His touch and voice and compassion untied her, and she immediately stood up straight and began praising God.

Unlike the woman with the bleeding disorder, this woman did not ask Jesus to heal her, and she did not demonstrate faith in him. This healing was completely at his initiative. She does not speak in Luke's account and we do not know what she was thinking. She is not the main character in this story. The point is that Jesus performs a healing miracle, and then men fight about it. Why?

Jesus had broken a rule, and the leader of the synagogue was indignant. Healing was forbidden on the Sabbath, because healing was work, and work was prohibited. Jesus could have healed the woman on any other day of the week. Why break the Sabbath? If she had been bent over for eighteen long years, what was one more day?

The leader of the synagogue had a valid point. The Jewish people observed the Sabbath because God observed the Sabbath. God created the world in six days (Gen. 1), and on the seventh day God took time off to rest. God chose not to work all the time. God then gave the gift of rest to God's people so they would not have to work all the time. But the Israelites had a hard time figuring out how to do Sabbath. There were always questions. What was work? Was it work to carry something? How far could they walk? So they developed rules to help them keep the Sabbath. And rules to help them keep the rules. And soon people remembered the rules but forgot the reason for the rules, which was to rest, relax, and enjoy God's good creation.

Jesus was also indignant, but not about broken rules. He was angry that Satan had bound the woman and caused her disease. And he was angry at the man who favored rules over people. Jesus argued that mercy and healing were more important than keeping a rule. He drew on a religious precedent. The rules said that anyone who had a thirsty animal could untie it and lead it to water, even on the Sabbath. Untying the animal was work, but it was a work of mercy and therefore acceptable. If you can be kind to your animal, Jesus said, how much more legitimate is it to be kind to this woman held in bondage by Satan for eighteen years? Why wait one day more if he could heal her today?

The woman's disability would have kept her on the margins all those years, tiptoeing around the edges of the worship space and the marketplace. She probably longed to be seen, acknowledged, and recognized, but at the same time she hoped no one would notice or shame her. When he healed her, Jesus addressed her as a daughter of Abraham, the founding father of the Israelite people. The name signaled that she belonged. With these words, Jesus put her back in the center. Jesus named, acknowledged, saw her. She was no longer an outsider or someone to be feared. She fully belonged to the family of God.

Diving Deeper

Jesus saw her. Jesus noticed the woman and did not react with disgust. He saw her, and he responded. It is easy to become blind to people we would prefer not to see, whether they are homeless, or panhandling, or disabled, or people of a different race or ethnicity. If you ride public transportation or live in a big city, you may have trained yourself not to make eye contact. Not to notice. Because how could you have compassion for all those people?

Every once in a while we are struck by the exceptions. Amy waited for a train on a crowded platform. When she finally found a seat and settled in, she realized she did not have her phone. She rushed back to where she had been waiting and asked people if they had seen her phone. She was desperate and panicky, as most of us would be. Not only are phones expensive to replace, but much of our essential life information is on our phones. Finally another woman on the platform offered to call Amy's phone so that the ringing might help her locate it. In the midst of her panic, Amy reflected later, "This woman saw me." The woman recognized her desperation and was kind to her. Amy never did find her phone, which had been stolen, but that moment reminded her that people could be kind. And that it is a gift to be seen and cared for.

She stood up straight. Jesus said, "Woman, you are set free from your ailment" (Luke 13:12). He touched her, and she immediately stood up straight and praised God. Her disease had tied her up in knots. Jesus untied the knots and set her free from bondage.

Jesus might speak similar words through a pastor, a therapist, or a friend. The healing words might include these phrases: "It was not your fault." "You are enough." "You are gifted." "You belong." "You can." "You can overcome." "You are wise." "You are kind." Sometimes freedom from bondage can happen quickly if there is an "aha!" moment or a sudden shift, but more often, standing up straight takes time. The longer the bondage continued (years of physical or emotional abuse, for example), the longer it might take to be loosed from it.

Looking back on the various kinds of bondage listed above, what might it mean to be set free from them? For some of the large social problems, such as foot-binding, female cutting, and Jim Crow laws, it takes a village to set people free. People have had to speak up, over and over, sometimes at great personal cost, to challenge the indignities of racism and sexism and other forms of dehumanization and exclusion. A good supply of righteous anger is usually required.

Melinda Gates tells the story of Kakenya Ntaiya, a Kenyan woman whose future of early marriage and endless chores had been set out for her by her family and by custom. She did not want to be constantly bound to cleaning, cooking, farming, and fetching water and wood.

She said no. She agreed to the ritual genital cutting, but in exchange for following that tradition, she told her family that she wanted to go to school. After finishing college, she returned to her village and started schools for girls. Gates observes, "Change starts when someone says 'No!'"[9]

Sometimes change happens when people say yes. In 2019, the Churchwide Assembly of the Evangelical Lutheran Church in America celebrated three anniversaries: the fiftieth anniversary of the ordination of women, the fortieth anniversary of the ordination of a woman of color, and the tenth anniversary of officially ordaining LGBTQ+ people. Before these changes, prospective ELCA clergy were bound by the church rules that excluded them and said no to their sense of call. Finally, the ELCA said yes! The rules were changed and the marginalized were included. On this festive anniversary occasion, two hundred women in their clergy robes and stoles processed into the room. Some danced. Some fist-pumped. The whole ELCA celebrated the gifts that formerly marginalized and excluded people had brought to the denomination. Not only were they standing up straight, they were dancing for joy!

Indignant. Jesus was indignant at suffering and indifference to suffering. What are we indignant at? What makes our blood boil? There has been so much to be indignant at lately. The shootings at the Pulse nightclub in Orlando. The Easter bombings in Sri Lanka. Attacks on synagogues and churches. Refugees in cages. Two mass shootings in twenty-four hours. A gun that can kill or injure thirty people in thirty seconds. We are exhausted. There is not enough energy to be indignant at everything that deserves our fury.

What do we do with that indignation? We can channel it into action, whether that be protests or volunteering or contacting our member of Congress. It is hard work to keep persisting together.

Belonging. The woman was an outcast. She was seen as sinful and undesirable because of her illness. Every culture and community has its outsiders, whether they are poor, or immigrants, or people of a different faith or race or ethnic group. Melinda Gates notes that in her work with women around the world, it is important to bring everyone, even people of the lowest caste, back into the community. But that is not enough. She writes, "We have to wake up to the ways we exclude. We have to open our arms and our hearts to the people we've pushed to the margins. It's not enough to help outsiders fight their way in—the real triumph will come when we no longer push anyone out."[10]

How has the church pushed people out? How have religious people marginalized those who are not religious? What would it look like for the church to be fully welcoming?

Questions for Reflection and Discussion

How have you felt bound or weighed down or bent over? What was the cause of that feeling for you? How have you felt set free?

What do you do with your anger and indignation? Write? Protest? Speak? Organize?

How can the church participate in healing and transforming? How can the church say no to oppression and yes to liberation?

3

The Outcasts

THE SYRO-PHOENICIAN WOMAN
(Mark 7:24–30*)

If hundreds of people lined up for a glimpse of you, if they wanted to shake your hand or have a brief conversation, or if they wanted to ask you a favor or take a selfie, would you be energized? Or exhausted by the mere thought of it? Your answer may reveal whether you are an extrovert who draws energy from people or an introvert who is replenished by solitude.

Consider the members of the British royal family who attend events where hundreds of people wait for a glimpse, an acknowledgment, a handshake. Extroverts might thrive on those activities. Introverts, whether they are royals, teachers, or preachers, can often perform well enough in groups, but they are likely exhausted afterward and eager to be alone.

I wonder if Jesus was an introvert. There were always so many hurting people touching him, begging for a moment of his time, or asking for healing. Jesus also spent hours in conversation with the clueless disciples, who did not understand his mission and ministry. Jesus was present for all these people. He paid attention. He cared for them. He gave them the healing and the wisdom and the affirmation that they

---

* The story of the Syro-Phoenician woman also appears in Matthew 15:21–28.

sought. But in this story, he was tired. He left the crowds and went to a quiet place where he could be alone to rest and recharge.

He went to a town where more Gentiles than Jews lived, hoping no one would recognize him as a healer. Gentiles were non-Jewish people. For most of their history, Jews had kept their distance from Gentiles, who were considered different, dangerous, and undesirable. The Jews were God's chosen people. The Gentiles were not.

Even in a Gentile town, Jesus could not escape notice. A Gentile woman learned where he was staying and came to ask a favor. This woman is labeled Syro-Phoenician in Mark and Canaanite in Matthew. She was an outsider. She would not be considered one of God's chosen people. But she was a mother on a mission; she did not care much about religious and ethnic identities. Her daughter was ill with what was then called demon possession. Now the disease might be labeled epilepsy or mental illness.

The woman had been watching Jesus from a distance. He had a caring presence and a gentleness about him. He did not shake one hand while looking ahead to the next person in line. He looked people in the eye and gave them his full attention. He was compassionate. People felt important and valued around him. Healing was not a business for Jesus. He did not demand adulation or payment. She had been watching from a distance. But now Jesus was in her neighborhood.

The woman took a risk approaching Jesus. It would have been more socially acceptable if the girl's father, grandfather, or uncle had made this request. But if there was a man in this family unit, he was not asking any favors for the girl. The mother had to make the request herself.

She knew she would be out of place and out of line if she asked a man for a favor, but she thought of her daughter's pain and isolation and told herself that it couldn't hurt to ask. At worst, he would say no. She went to the house he had entered and fell down at his feet, a typical sign of humility and gratitude. She may have intended to be rational and respectful, but her words tumbled out. "Please, sir, I know you are very busy, but I see that you heal people and I wondered if you could help my daughter who is very sick." Then she waited. Jesus looked at her for a long time, and it was not a comfortable silence. Finally he said, "Let the children be fed first, for it is not fair to take the children's food and throw it to the dogs" (Mark 7:27).

She was stunned. What kind of answer was that? Was this gracious man calling her a dog? He was Jewish and she was not, but would he say no to her because of her ethnicity? Apparently he would! And harshly! She imagined the aggressive wild dogs that lived near the garbage dump and survived on scraps that people threw away. Was that how he thought of her? She felt humiliated and wanted to escape before he could humiliate her even further. She had badly misjudged him. He was not kind, but rude and dismissive, and there was no point in further conversation. She was not about to beg. She knew when she wasn't wanted.

Then she thought again of her daughter's discomfort and discouragement. She thought of the amazing power of healing Jesus possessed. She thought about the crowds of people who were constantly asking something from him, and she found a bit of empathy for Jesus. Of course he was tired and irritable. And maybe he had priorities she did not understand. She also thought of the affectionate dogs in her childhood home who were quick to gobble up any dropped crumb. Maybe it was not so insulting to be compared to a household pet. She tried to see the world through his eyes, but she also refused to give up and slink away quietly in disgrace and shame. She persisted. She talked back. She used his own words to reframe the situation. "Sir, even the dogs under the table eat the children's crumbs" (Mark 7:28).

The woman realized something Jesus may have forgotten in his weariness. There was enough grace and healing for all. She was willing to be in second place, willing to be compared to a dog while the Jewish people sat at the table, but she knew that even a crumb of Jesus' power was enough to heal her daughter.

Jesus listened to her response, even though he had just spoken harshly to her. When he listened, he realized that she was right. There was enough of God's power for all: Jew and Gentile, insider and outsider, children and dogs. He did not have to limit his healing ministry to the Jews.

This woman showed deep faith in him, despite his brush-off. She knew her daughter did not need to be in the same room with Jesus to be healed, because divine power was not limited to proximity. She believed in Jesus, even when he was not at his best. Jesus acknowledged her faith. "For saying that," he said, "you may go—the demon has left your daughter" (Mark 7:29).

What are we to make of this story, which shows Jesus in a negative light? The gentle Jesus seems a little snappy here. One commentator said that he was caught with his compassion down. He had run out of patience and refused to heal upon request. That seems completely out of character for Jesus.

Commentators and preachers have tried to find a good explanation for his behavior. Some claim that Jesus was testing the woman's faith. He intended to heal her daughter all along but wanted to see the depth of her trust. Some commentators suggest that he had a twinkle in his eye or a smile on his face, and insist that she knew he was testing or teasing her. The story, however, gives no evidence that Jesus winked, joked, or teased, only that he said no.

Is it possible that Jesus learned something from her? Perhaps he was still working out the details and recipients of his ministry and did not think it was the right time to expand beyond the Jews. He thought he needed to care for the Jews first, and he had not yet completed that work. Could she have helped him see differently? Did she convince him to change his mind? Did she show him that there was enough love and healing to go around to Jews and Gentiles?

Some people hesitate at this idea. They insist that Jesus was fully divine and knew everything. He did not need to be instructed by a Gentile woman, of all people! But Jesus was also fully human. This is one of the great mysteries of the Christian faith. Jesus is God-made-flesh, but he is also a human being, and human beings do not know everything. Jesus could grow and learn and change just as all humans do. When the woman challenged him to expand his view of ministry, he did not ignore or argue with her. Instead he demonstrated personal integrity, self-confidence, and willingness to learn from someone who was "beneath" him. It is not a sign of weakness to change our minds or expand our view of the world.

Diving Deeper

Reframing the story: When Jesus refused to heal her daughter, the woman's first instinct might have been to conclude that Jesus was right and she was wrong. She should not have bothered him. She was an outsider and her daughter was not worth healing. She might then have backed away muttering apologies. She might also have concluded that Jesus was not a healer but a crabby man who did not want to be bothered, and she should escape as quickly as possible.

Instead, she told herself a different story. She dealt with this awkward situation by reframing it. She found some empathy for Jesus. She took a put-down and turned it around. She did not conclude that she and her daughter were worthless. She did not conclude that Jesus was mean-spirited. Instead, she sensed his reluctance, his weariness, and his sense of mission, and she responded to those deeper concerns with creative empathy. She recognized that a dog could be a beloved member of the family rather than an angry wild dog at the trash dump.

We often make assumptions about what other people think. If a boss, spouse, child, friend, or coworker snaps at us, we might assume they dislike us or are angry because we have done something wrong. We tell ourselves a story to explain their behavior, but the real story may be completely different. The teenager may be bullied at school. The spouse may have had a bad day at work. The boss may be worried about the bottom line. How do we try to listen to the story people are not telling? To the pain that is driving the angry words?[1]

"*Nevertheless, she persisted.*" This phrase has become a bit of a cliché since a male US senator used it to criticize a female senator for refusing to sit down and be quiet. Still, it has resonated with a lot of people, and it is a good description of the woman in this story.

When we are ignored or patronized or criticized or demeaned, it is tempting to slink away and avoid further conflict, or to shut down and refuse to engage. Why waste our time with people who won't listen or don't understand? Why engage with people who call us dogs—or worse? This woman did not back down. She talked back to Jesus. She stayed in the conversation with him, and in the end, she helped him see differently. She persisted in the face of rejection because she believed in Jesus and wanted healing for her daughter.

Feminist theologian Elisabeth Schüssler Fiorenza has frequently criticized the Roman Catholic Church for its refusal to ordain women to the priesthood. She is often asked why she does not simply leave and attend another church, and she replies, "Because it is my church." Other people have disagreed with their denominations over women's ordination or same-sex marriage or racism, but rather than break the relationship, they have persisted. They believe that the denomination can be better, and more gracious, so they refuse to leave. Their persistence can be a gift.

The same is true for those who challenge their country's practices on race or immigration or taxation. Those who persistently criticize do so because they think the institution or the congregation or the nation needs to be true to its ideals. They call it back to its goals or its theology or its original intentions. Persistence can be a gift.

It is also important to know when to stop persisting and leave a difficult situation. Jesus was a worthy opponent who was willing to listen to this woman. Ideally, the church or the nation or the institution is a worthy opponent willing to listen to criticism and willing to change. Unfortunately, some opponents are not worthy and might do serious physical or emotional harm to those who persist. In situations where there is a threat, it may be better not to persist. It is not always easy to discern the difference.

Talking back to back talk. Jesus initially refused to heal the woman's daughter because Gentiles were not the priority of his ministry. She did not accept that answer, and she challenged him to be more inclusive. She reminded him that there was enough grace to go around. She talked back. Jesus listened to her, changed his mind, and healed her daughter as she asked.

What might Jesus have done instead? He might have dismissed her as an angry woman he could safely ignore. He might have shut the door in her face. He might have defended his approach to ministry and insisted she was wrong. Instead he listened, and he took her seriously.

How do we respond when someone talks back to us? Your partner or child might get frustrated and say harshly, "You never listen. You are always on your phone!" Or, "You're so negative." Those are hard words to hear, perhaps not framed in the most helpful way. How do we respond? Do we get angry and stomp away? Do we offer a countercharge about the other person's bad behavior? Do we accuse them of exaggerating? Or do we go quiet, take the criticism to heart, and conclude that this is more evidence that we are bad people, while still refusing to change our behavior?

What if we could listen to the back talk and try not to be so defensive? Some of the hardest but wisest words to say in these situations might be, "Can you tell me more?" Or, "You might be right." What if we could put ourselves in the other person's shoes and think about why they are criticizing us?

It is also difficult to hear someone accuse us of being narrow-minded or racist or sexist or homophobic. We can dismiss the criticism as hysterical or silly. We can leave the conversation and refuse to engage further. We can take the criticism as further evidence that we are bad people who have no power to change our bad behavior. These responses are common, normal, and human, but they do not promote healthy relationships.

When a person of color confronts a white person about white privilege, it is easy for the white person to get tense and angry and defensive. The white listeners might get their feelings hurt. Or insist that they are not racist. Or the listeners may take the criticism to heart and acknowledge the accusation and feel bad but not really repent or try to engage or make amends. But often those sharp, honest, direct words are exactly what privileged people need to hear and then act on.

What if we could be more open to people who disagreed with us? What if we assumed they have something to teach us, even if it is difficult? What if we did not shame them in response?

On a private Facebook group that discussed religious and church issues, a young, gay person of color often pointed out examples of discrimination and injustice in the broader church. He also sometimes confronted individuals for their comments that he considered racist, insensitive, or insufficiently supportive of marginalized people. There were some tense moments and some hard conversations, but his persistence helped people see how their words and actions affected others. They would have been unlikely to hear such criticism in their families and workplaces.

Lewis Smedes describes a friend who, on his deathbed, pointed out some flaws in Lewis that he hoped he would address. Smedes writes, "If you wonder where God's grace can be found, find yourself a critical friend. A friend who wants you to be as good a person as you can be, a friend who dares to confront your flaws and failures, and then accepts the whole of you in grace."[2]

Self-care and life-work balance. How do you manage all the demands in your life? How do you refill the energy tank after it is empty? Jesus is sometimes held up as a model of tireless and perpetual motion who constantly cared for people with never a thought for himself. Those who try to follow Jesus now are sometimes told that they should be equally selfless and hard-working. This story shows that Jesus did take time for self-care.

During my first year of graduate school I was also a full-time interim pastor. The congregation wanted me to stay and expressed a lot of appreciation, which was intoxicating. I told my adviser about my dilemma: I wanted to focus more fully on graduate work, but the church members said they liked me as their pastor. My adviser smiled and said, "You're not indispensable, you know."

I have remembered those words numerous times in the last thirty years when I have been tempted to take on yet another committee or "opportunity." We all have a lot of demands on our time and energy: work, aging parents, young children, church, volunteering. Much of it is good and important. But we are not indispensable, and we are called to care for ourselves as Jesus cared for himself.

Questions for Reflection and Discussion

If you are dealing with a difficult situation, how do you know how long to persist? How do you know when to leave a toxic situation?

How have you dealt with critics? How do you offer criticism or a rebuttal or disagreement? How do you discern when criticism is valid and when it is not?

Do you think Jesus could have changed his mind? What does it mean for Jesus to be both human and divine?

The woman suggested to Jesus that there was enough grace to go around for everyone. Do you believe that? Are there limits to God's grace?

THE SAMARITAN WOMAN
(John 4)

Consider how the story of the Samaritan woman might sound if Jesus were traveling in Texas today.

Jesus and his disciples were passing through El Paso on the way to San Antonio. The disciples left Jesus in the center of town and went to the store to buy groceries. Jesus was too hungry to wait, so he went to a food truck and bought some rice and beans. He started talking (in fluent Spanish) with the woman who worked in the truck. She was an undocumented immigrant from Guatemala. Jesus said the food was great. "Do you run this all by yourself?" "Well," she said, "that's a long story." "I have time," Jesus said.

"I have a partner. He owns the truck. I do the cooking and selling."

Jesus said, "I'm guessing it is more complicated than that."

"Yes," she said. "I work really hard, but he doesn't pay me. Whenever I ask him for my wages, he threatens to turn me in to the immigration authorities."

"Is there anyone else you can go to?" Jesus asked.

"No. I have a son. He is in school. And he has asthma, and there is a clinic here that helps him for free."

"How did you end up with this man?" Jesus asked.

"I was desperate to find a place to live. I was with a man who was beating me, so I had to leave. Before that I was with a man I really loved, who was kind to me, but he got deported. I had never married him because I'm married to a man in Guatemala. He was put in prison fifteen years ago. I left then, because I was afraid I would be put in prison too."

"I'm sorry," Jesus said. "That is a difficult life."

Then the disciples came back and wondered why he was talking to a Latina woman who ran a food truck. But they said nothing, because Jesus was always hanging out with unexpected people.

In August 2019, a young man targeted Latinos at a Wal-Mart in El Paso and killed twenty-two people. Later in the week, hundreds of undocumented workers were taken from meat processing plants in Mississippi, leaving their young children alone to fend for themselves. These are only two of multiple incidents of oppression of brown-skinned immigrants. They have been demonized, dehumanized, and told to go back to where they came from. It is not America's finest hour.

Samaritans in the first century were comparable to Latino and Muslim immigrants in the United States in the twenty-first century. Samaritans were probably treated better, but certainly not well. Samaritans were despised, feared, and avoided. But Jesus had an encounter with a Samaritan woman who turned out to be both theologically perceptive and a very good evangelist.

Jesus and the disciples are traveling through Samaria. The disciples go off to buy food, and Jesus meets a Samaritan woman and asks her for a drink. With this simple request, Jesus defies two religious taboos. A Jewish man was not supposed to have a conversation with a woman who was not his wife. And Jews were not supposed to talk to or ask favors of Samaritans.

Understanding the significance of this encounter requires some background information about the relationship between Jews and Samaritans, who had a long history of disagreement and conflict. The nation of Israel experienced its most successful time during the rule of King David, but only two generations later, the nation had split in two. The southern kingdom retained Jerusalem, the center of Jewish worship life. The northern kingdom did not have a similarly significant place of worship. In 722 BCE, the northern kingdom was invaded by Assyria, and many of the Israelites were carried off into captivity. Those who remained intermarried with their captors and other "foreigners," which meant that they were considered racially impure. At times they adopted the deities and worship practices of other nations (as the Jews in the southern kingdom also did), and thus were considered religiously impure also. These northern kingdom people became known as Samaritans. They built a worship space on Mount Gerizim in the northern part of Israel, but in 128 BCE this temple was destroyed by Jewish forces. By the time of Jesus, the Samaritans and Jews had a long history of mutual dislike, distrust, and disgust. The Jewish attempt to maintain distance and avoid impurity was so extreme that Jews walking from Galilee south to Jerusalem would travel many miles out of their way to avoid passing through Samaria.

The disciples are probably quite surprised, then, when Jesus chooses to travel through Samaria rather than around it. When they reach the well where Jacob met Rachel (Gen. 29), Jesus chooses to stay there while the disciples go to buy groceries. A Samaritan woman comes to the well to draw water. Jesus is thirsty, but he has no bucket to draw water, so he asks the woman for a drink. She is shocked, because a good Jewish man would never drink from a Samaritan woman's bucket. Samaritans in general, and Samaritan women in particular, were considered impure and dangerous. Jews would not eat their food or use their utensils for fear of "catching" Samaritan sin. She asks point-blank why Jesus would ask her for water.

An odd and meandering conversation follows, full of symbols and metaphors. Jesus says that if she knew who he was, she would ask him for "living water." She takes him literally and assumes that he knows of a spring or a stream that would provide fresh running water rather than the stagnant water from the well. She does not understand that Jesus is speaking metaphorically about a new kind of life and sustenance that he could provide for her. She is curious, even though she does not quite follow him. The living water sounds appealing.

Jesus then suggests that she go home and bring her husband back with her. She replies that she has no husband. That's true, Jesus says, and observes that she has had five husbands and the man she is currently living with is not her husband. She is surprised that he knows this about her and concludes that he must be a prophet because he can perceive what is not obvious. She sees an opportunity to ask this wise and perceptive man a question that was at the heart of the tension between Jews and Samaritans. Jews insist that God must be worshiped in Jerusalem, she says, but Samaritans worship in their own place on Mount Gerizim. Who is right?

Jesus takes her question seriously, and his answer transcends the centuries of debate and conflict. The time is coming, he said, when people will worship God "in spirit and truth." The location will no longer matter, and God's people will be united in their faith. The woman says that she believes a messiah is coming who will make this happen. Jesus then tells her astounding news: he is the Messiah she is expecting. Jesus was rarely this explicit about his messianic identity, but here he chooses to make a dramatic and significant statement about himself to a woman who was considered impure and even dangerous.

At that point the disciples return and are astonished to find him speaking with a woman, but they say nothing. The woman leaves her water jar behind, just as the other disciples who followed Jesus left behind their fishing nets, boats, jobs, and families. She returns to her town and invites everyone, not just the man she lives with, "Come and see a man who told me everything I have ever done! He cannot be the Messiah, can he?" (John 4:29). She must have been very persuasive and passionate, because they all return to Jesus with her. Jesus teaches them, and they believe and acknowledge him as the Savior of the world. She functioned much like John the Baptist, Andrew, and Philip, who brought people to Jesus (John 1).

In this story, Jesus conveys good news to an unexpected group of people, but his actions would not have been popular at the time. How could Jesus offer salvation to the despised Samaritans? That was the trouble with Jesus. He did not follow the rules. He stepped into the history of dislike, distrust, and disgust, and did things differently. He engaged in theological conversation with a Samaritan woman who would have been considered incapable of it. He took her seriously, and he respectfully answered her questions. He extended grace to her and to her neighbors; he invited them to participate in his work, and he announced that he was their Messiah too.

He overcame the worship wars between Jews and Samaritans by suggesting that they worshiped the same God and the disagreement about location was less important than their common faith. Jesus showed radical inclusivity and good news for all, and this encounter began to heal the breach between two groups of people with a common history and a shared faith.

This is a powerful, positive story in which a woman engages with Jesus and then plays a significant role in evangelizing her community. She is sent out with the good news, just as the apostles were sent out with the good news of Jesus in the early church.

You may have heard a very different analysis in sermons or Bible studies.[3] This story has a long history of interpretation that criticizes the Samaritan woman. She has been labeled a slut, a whore, a sinful woman, an adulteress. Much has been written about her having five husbands, as if she were Elizabeth Taylor, the actress who was married eight times to seven men. One commentator called the Samaritan woman a five-time loser.[4] Others wondered how many husbands she deserted and how many left her because she was unfaithful or failed to do her duties.

She is also criticized for her questions about living water and the proper location for worship. Jesus was speaking in metaphors, which are confusing to contemporary readers, but some commentators insist that she failed to understand these difficult words because she was a stubborn, sinful woman who had to be confronted with the truth. She was not engaging in a thoughtful theological discussion with Jesus, but trying to evade his probing into her sinful life. He was too smart for her and refused to be redirected.

Several commentators also minimize her intelligence. They do not think she was smart enough to ask about the location of worship. One commentator writes: "We may still wonder if a Samaritan woman would have been expected to understand even the most basic ideas of the discourse." He labels her as "markedly immoral" and describes her behavior as "mincing and coy."[5]

Edith Deen, in *All of the Women of the Bible*, imagines that the Samaritan woman was not only bad and stupid but also ugly. Deen claims that she had once been pretty, but after a life lived for carnal pleasure, she was now sad and hard. Her once voluptuous body was old and weary.[6] None of these speculations are supported by the story!

Commentators also have made claims about Jesus that are not present in the text. One commentator argues that "Jesus accuses her of a life of loose morals,"[7] but Jesus actually said nothing about her situation except to name it. He did not accuse or shame her. The interpretation of his words depends on his tone of voice. He could have been sarcastic and snarky: "Yeah, you've had *five* husbands and you aren't married to the guy you are with now. You are such a loser." This is not how Jesus typically responds. Or he could have spoken to her in a calm voice that gave the impression of sympathy and compassion. "You've had a tough time with relationships, haven't you?" Rather than accusing or chastising her, Jesus seems to affirm that he sees her and knows her as she is. She responds by acknowledging his ability to see her life.

These critical commentators ignore the cultural and historical context of the story. It is highly unlikely that she would have been able to marry and divorce five husbands on her own. She may have been repeatedly widowed, divorced, or abandoned. She may have been forced into a series of levirate marriages, if she was left childless when her first husband died, and one brother after another was compelled to marry her.[8] It may not have been sin at all, but rather bad luck or bad men, that led to her multiple marriages. The Samaritan woman would not have had the freedom of Liz Taylor to marry and quickly divorce multiple husbands. The man she was living with might have refused to marry her out of fear that he too would die. Or she may have been desperately poor and chose to live with a man who would support her even if he refused to marry her. She may not have had many options to support herself.

Perhaps she is criticized so harshly because some commentators would prefer to dismiss her as a sinful woman rather than take her seriously the way that Jesus did. Jesus revealed himself to her as the Messiah, even though she was perceived by some religious people as a loser, a sinner, a reject, a danger. He entrusted her with good news that she then shared. She functioned as the apostles did after the resurrection. Maybe that is too threatening! If Jesus takes her seriously as a conversation partner and as an evangelist or preacher, maybe all women need to be taken seriously.

The details of her sexual and marital history ultimately do not matter. The point of the story is that she and Jesus talked, he taught her, and she was astute and perceptive. She asked good questions. She was a member of a despised group yet showed an interest in Jesus, a willingness to care for him, and a kind of intuitive sense about him and his ministry. She was a Samaritan and a woman, and she may have had a reputation, and yet she recognized Jesus as someone special and shared that news with others. She was not a naive bimbo but an intelligent, thoughtful, curious woman who was not constrained by her past or her reputation. She proclaimed the gospel to her community even if she was not absolutely certain about all the details. ("He cannot be the Messiah, can he?") Like the apostles after the resurrection, she enthusiastically shared the news about her encounter with Jesus, a man who somehow changed everything.

Diving Deeper

He told me everything I'd ever done. Did she experience this word from Jesus as judgment? Or as empathy and compassion? It depends a bit on his tone of voice, but Jesus seems to be saying that he knows her situation but she does not have to be defined by it. She initially tries to downplay her situation by saying, "I have no husband" (which was probably the truth, and not necessarily an evasion). But Jesus knows, and he states the reality of the five husbands and the current awkward situation. And when he says that matter-of-factly and without judgment, she can move on. She can find some freedom. She can cut loose from the shame that is weighing her down. She is known, not judged. Jesus sees her.

If you were fully known by someone else, would that feel like judgment or liberation to you? It depends on the complexity of our past! It depends on the character and integrity of the knower.

How do we move on so that we are no longer defined by our actions in the past?

Repentance or healing? Is she a sinner who needs to be humiliated so that she will repent? Or is she a person suffering from shame who needs to be healed and affirmed? Jesus does confront people for hypocrisy, legalism, greed, and other sins. But when he encounters people (usually women) with bad reputations, he is compassionate rather than confrontational. He understands their situations. He treats them as more sinned against than sinful.

"Come and see." The Samaritan woman shares the good news with her community. She does not wait for approval or authorization. She was an evangelist. Evangelism in our context often has a bad reputation. We might think about people who show up at the front door at dinnertime and want to debate religion. Her sharing of the good news about Jesus must have conveyed a sense of discovery, affirmation, and deep joy. How do we convey that without being "that person" who is always talking weirdly about Jesus? What are examples of positive and negative evangelism?

"Astonished that he was speaking with a woman." In the first century, speaking with a woman was a significant taboo for a Jewish man. Who are the marginalized people today who are treated with dislike, distrust, and disgust? Why? That is a very significant question. What is it about some groups of people that makes them so disliked? Do you know people from those groups? How do you explain your feelings toward them? What is the influence of education, religion, the media?

Does the way that Jesus treats marginalized people have an impact on the way you think about people?

Questions for Reflection and Discussion

When have you felt shamed? What has helped to heal that?

When have you felt known and understood?

What are the theological questions you wish Jesus could answer for you?

What needs to be forgiven, in your life and in the world? What needs to be healed?

THE WOMAN CAUGHT IN ADULTERY
(John 8:1–11)

Imagine you are watching a cable news show after a politician has been caught in a scandal involving money, sex, or power. After several minutes of the usual harrumphing and tut-tutting from the pundits, one of them piously quotes a saying of Jesus: "Let anyone among you who is without sin be the first to throw a stone" (John 8:7). This show of tolerance and sensitivity appears to shut down further criticism, as everyone agrees that no one is without sin. This nonjudgmental attitude seems admirable, but is that what Jesus meant? Should all behavior be free from judgment?

The way Jesus treated sinful people was one of the controversial aspects of his ministry. The saying mentioned above comes from a story in John's Gospel in which Jesus is asked what to do about a sinful woman. Jesus was a popular teacher, and some of the religious leaders resented his popularity and influence, so they developed a plan to make trouble for him. One morning when Jesus was teaching in the temple in Jerusalem, the religious leaders brought a woman to Jesus and claimed she had been "caught in the very act of committing adultery" (8:4). The leaders asked Jesus what should be done with the woman, reminding him that the Jewish law said that such women should be stoned. This was a trap. If Jesus said she should be set free, he would be denying Jewish religious law and appear to be soft on sin. If Jesus agreed that she should be executed, he could get in trouble with the Roman government for meddling in legal affairs. The religious leaders were trying to find a way to charge him with religious or political lawbreaking. Either way, he would be wrong. It was a no-win situation. Especially for the woman.

She was a pawn in this power struggle between men. She was dragged into the temple and put on display as a vile, disgusting creature who had given in to lust and dishonored her husband by sleeping with another man. But something was missing. If she had been caught in the act of adultery, where was the man? If it takes two to tango, why wasn't her lover dragged before the authorities?

What if there was no lover? What if the sexual encounter was not loving and mutual, but violent and forced? She may have been a maid forced into sexual activity by her employer. She may have run an inn with her husband, and a patron forced himself on her in an empty courtyard. Perhaps her husband no longer wanted her, so he arranged for someone to rape her and pretend it was adultery. What if it was a setup engineered by the religious leaders solely to put Jesus in an awkward situation?

The definition of adultery in biblical times was not the same for men and women. A married man who slept with another woman did not sin against his wife, because he owned her. The wife had no right to expect her husband to remain faithful to her. A man could not have sex with a married woman, because she belonged to another man. He could not have sex with a virgin, because she belonged to her father, who guarded her purity until she married. A married man could sleep with women who did not belong to a man—prostitutes, for example, and possibly widows and servants. A married woman who engaged in illicit sex disobeyed and insulted her husband, who owned her. If a man had sex with a married woman, both were guilty and deserved punishment.

It is certainly possible that the woman had chosen to engage in a relationship with someone not her husband, but it is odd that the man would not have been brought in also. Jewish law said clearly, "If a man is caught lying with the wife of another man, both of them shall die" (Deut. 22:22; Lev. 20:10). If the man was not brought in, he may have been a participant in a setup. Perhaps she was falsely accused.

Whatever the exact circumstances, the woman was little more than an object that the religious leaders used to set their trap for Jesus.

Nobody cared about her welfare. Nobody asked about the identity or whereabouts of her partner. Nobody wondered if there might be extenuating circumstances. The point was to get Jesus. If she was stoned in the process, nobody seemed to care.

The religious leaders pressed Jesus to make an immediate decision about her fate. The law said she should be stoned. Should they kill her immediately? Their questions seem bloodthirsty, as if they were eager to dig a hole in which she would stand while they hurled stones at her head. They were equally eager to trap Jesus in a moral dilemma and watch him squirm.

The crowd watched the men debate the terrified woman's future while she remained silent. There was no trial. She was not considered innocent until proven guilty. She had no right to defend herself or hire a lawyer. The crowd watched and wondered what Jesus would do.

Jesus simply refused to choose. The religious leaders presented Jesus with an impossible choice, a no-win situation, but he did not accept the flawed terms of debate. Instead of answering, he bent over and began writing in the dirt. Some commentators have suggested that he was writing the sins of the accusers. That is a possibility, but the content of the writing probably was not as significant as the fact that Jesus ignored them! He refused to play the game by the rules the religious leaders set out. They set a trap to challenge his authority, but he did not allow himself to be caught.

This was a strategy of active resistance. Jesus was not undecided or afraid. He refused to get caught up in the accusers' dysfunction. Jesus kept himself differentiated, to use a psychological term. It was as if he said, in the contemporary phrase, "Not my circus. Not my monkeys."

As Jesus wrote on the ground, the scribes and Pharisees continued to badger him. When he finally stood up, he deftly put the situation back in their court without confronting them directly. He said, "Let anyone among you who is without sin be the first to throw a stone at her" (John 8:7). Then he did some more writing on the ground, avoiding eye contact. Jesus did not berate or shame the men. He did not preach a fire-and-brimstone sermon outlining their sins. He did not excuse them. He challenged them to look honestly at themselves and assess their behavior. One by one, the men slipped away, beginning with the oldest. Finally Jesus stood up and saw that he and the woman were alone. "Has no one condemned you?" he asked. "No one, sir," she said. Jesus said, "Neither do I condemn you. Go your way, and from now on do not sin again" (John 8:10–11). The Greek word translated "condemn" here (*katakrinō*) has a harsh meaning, "condemn to death or punishment." That is what the religious leaders wanted him to do to her, but he refused.

Confronted with someone about whom he might have assumed the worst, Jesus was remarkably gracious. He did not shame or belittle her. He set her free from judgment. He gave her a fresh start and the opportunity to redefine herself.

The good news in this story is the power of healing. Jesus says, to the woman and to us, I do not condemn you. I am not writing you off as hopelessly bad or sinful. If you made an unwise choice about a sexual partner, you can make better choices in the future. If you have been blamed or shamed for something that was not your fault, you need not accept the social judgment. If you were sexually assaulted, it was not your fault. If you were condemned as a slut or a whore or an adulterer, Jesus says, "I do not condemn you." Those names do not define you. You can start again.

So if Jesus does not condemn her, does that mean he does not condemn anyone? Are the pundits from the opening paragraph right in saying that they can't criticize anyone's bad behavior?

Jesus does not condemn the men, in the sense of labeling them as terrible, shameful human beings, but he does confront them. He encourages the men to see themselves clearly, come to terms with their own sin, and take responsibility for the ways they have behaved badly. When Jesus says, "Let anyone among you who is without sin be the first to throw a stone," it is not an excuse. It is not a way to let guilty people off the hook, with the excuse that everybody sins. Instead, it is an invitation to be honest about our own failings, in contrast to flabby admissions that "mistakes were made" or "I only did as I was told."

Jesus is not interested in condemning sexual sin, if indeed that is what the woman had done. He recognizes that the women caught in sexual sin may not have had a choice. He is far more critical of people who present themselves as pure and upright even though they may have committed the more "respectable" sins of hypocrisy, greed, judgment, and bigotry.

Diving Deeper

Seeing differently. I have read and taught this story numerous times and always assumed that the sexual relationship was mutual and that both people had consented to sexual activity. If the story referred to adultery, then what happened must have been adultery.

When I reread the story recently, I saw it through a different lens. In what has become known as the #MeToo movement, hundreds of women and some men have told stories of sexual harassment and assault. A doctor assaulted dozens of gymnasts but called his actions medical treatment. Famous men in the media, sports, and higher education were called out for unacceptable behavior. The church was not immune; dozens of stories emerged of priests, pastors, and other church employees who sexually assaulted women, boys, and girls. Victims said no, but were still assaulted. At times the power differential was clear. A young gymnast, an altar server, a student, an employee, or a child is not able to consent to sexual activity with someone who has power or authority over them. Other relationships might look mutual, but still lack full consent. A couple might agree to have dinner together, but if one pressures the other to have sex, using physical or emotional intimidation or "encouragement," that encounter is no longer mutual but qualifies as date rape.

Given all that had happened, when I read the story about the woman taken in adultery, I wondered whether it was not adultery but rape. The text does not give enough information to know for certain. But new lenses lead to new questions, which are worth asking. What if she was set up? What if she did not consent?

Is it legitimate for current events to reshape the lenses through which we read the Bible? I would argue that it is not only legitimate, but inevitable. When we look at the stories in different ways, we find that they resonate with our lives in different ways.

The Bible does not answer, or even address, many of our contemporary questions about sex and power. But the Bible offers larger principles. First, everyone is a human being made in God's image and is worthy of respect and dignity. Children, employees, students, immigrants, service workers. Everyone. Second, Jesus models kind and respectful treatment of other people. He might give this advice: "Listen to people when they speak. Do not force, humiliate, violate, or mistreat them. They are not there for anyone's sexual gratification, or as pawns for the powerful. Treat people with kindness, respect, and dignity." This is what Jesus cares about.

Cheap grace? In the opening paragraph of this chapter, I asked if this story might promote an easy forgiveness that excuses bad behavior without requiring repentance or restitution. This is sometimes called "cheap grace." Jesus appeared to easily forgive the woman without requiring her to repent or do penance for her sins. Some of the early Christian writers feared that women might think they could get away with adultery because Jesus would not condemn them for it.[9] Jesus was too nice, or "soft on sin."

You may notice that the story is in brackets in your Bible. It was not included in the earliest manuscripts of the Gospel of John.[10] Scholars wonder if one of the reasons it did not appear sooner was that the story made the church uneasy. They were not certain Jesus would have said such a thing and forgiven so easily.

But the story is much loved, perhaps precisely because it is so nice. Perhaps we are comforted by the belief that if Jesus forgave the sinful woman, he will forgive us too. It may be even more encouraging to know that Jesus sees the subtle but destructive sins of injustice, judgment, and hypocrisy, and refuses to excuse them.

"Neither do I condemn you." To condemn someone is to pass a harsh sentence that also carries a heavy load of shame. Historically the Christian church has spent a great deal of energy condemning women for their sexuality, especially when it is seen as a distraction or a temptation to men. Women have at times been harshly punished for sexual sins, in part because women can't hide a pregnancy, while men can deny or hide their role in it. In Nathaniel Hawthorne's *The Scarlet Letter*, Hester Prynne is forced to wear a scarlet *A* on her chest to signify her sin of adultery. Until the 1960s, in some congregations an unmarried pregnant woman might be forced to make a public confession of her sin, while the father was absent.

Condemnation occurs outside the church as well, though it may be more subtle. Consider dress codes in elementary school that don't allow eight-year-old girls to wear tank tops in a sweltering school building because their collarbones might distract the eight-year-old boys! Consider women forced to wear robes that cover their bodies and their faces. In so many ways, women have been condemned for having bodies, being sexual, and looking pretty.

Jesus seems to understand that much of what looked like sexual sin was actually women being taken advantage of and mistreated. In contrast to common practices of his time, Jesus was not afraid of women. He did not view them as temptresses. He respected them as full human beings.

Jesus rarely condemns people who are already at the bottom of society, but he does not tolerate bad behavior. He makes judgments, particularly on those sins that damage the well-being of the community, such as greed, abuse of power, and abuse of people. He criticizes the wealthy people who hoard their excess rather than use it to help others. He criticizes those who think they are defending religious rules and purity. Jesus did not simply say to these people (usually men), I do not condemn you, go and sin no more. He confronted them. He said their behavior was unacceptable.

If Jesus were around today, he might have some questions about the American system of justice. He might ask why those with an addiction to opioids receive sympathy and rehabilitation, while those addicted to crack or methamphetamines are sent to prison. Jesus might wonder why a white television star who pays a big bribe to get her child admitted into a university receives a fourteen-day jail sentence, while an African American homeless woman who lies about her address to get her child into a better school district gets five years in prison. Could it be that the justice system is flawed and biased?

That's the trouble with Jesus. He asks those hard questions. And he wants his followers to ask them too.

Questions for Reflection and Discussion

Can you think of examples of current events that might provide different lenses for reading the Bible?

Why are sexual sins, especially among women, so often considered worse sins, more dirty and disgusting than other sins? What sins receive less condemnation, and perhaps even some admiration?

How have you seen women being condemned for being women?

Where do you see the good news in this story?

Is it possible to differentiate as well as Jesus did? How do you decide when and how to act? To confront? To keep silent? How do you stay free of someone's mean-spirited agenda?

What in you might need recognition? Healing? Confronting?

4

The Grateful

THE WOMAN WHO ANOINTED JESUS
(Mark 14:3–9*)

Imagine wanting to do something nice for someone you care about. You cook an elaborate meal and clean the house, but that does not seem like enough, so you also remodel your home and scrub the streets. All told, you spend a year's salary.

How would you feel if you were the recipient of such generosity? Awkward and embarrassed? Or honored and valued?

Imagine that you are a man sitting at a dinner party with friends. A woman enters the room, approaches your seat, cracks open the neck of a large bottle of expensive perfumed oil, and pours the entire bottle over your head! The scent of the perfumed oil is strong and appealing without being overwhelming, and it masks all the bad human smells, along with the smells of onions and garlic and the animals just outside the door. The oil is a bit messy. It has soaked your hair and is running down your face and neck and into your clothes. But the room that moments ago smelled of body odor and chickens now smells like an elegant salon.

How would you feel if you were the recipient of such an act? Awkward and embarrassed? Or honored and valued because of an extraordinary act of generosity?

---

* The story of the woman who anointed Jesus also appears in Matthew 26:1–13.

The woman in this story gave an extravagant gift to Jesus to demonstrate her love and gratitude. The text does not explain how she knew Jesus or why she felt such love for him. She wanted to do something generous for him, so she bought a bottle of perfumed oil, worth a year's pay, and poured it on his head. It was an odd and messy thing to do.

We might feel awkward and embarrassed if this happened to us, but Jesus took it in stride. He did not say, "Oh, you shouldn't have." He did not cringe or withdraw from her. He did not look at her with disgust. He said nothing to shame her, even though her action was intimate, extravagant, pungent, and strange.

Some of the guests at the dinner (Matthew identifies them as the disciples; Mark does not specify) indignantly objected to the extravagance and complained that she had wasted money which should have been given to the poor. Did the critics actually care about the poor? Or were they embarrassed that she had given Jesus an expensive gift and they had not even brought a card? Perhaps they resented the intimacy of her action and considered it inappropriate. Perhaps they were jealous that she had this idea before they did. But rather than acknowledge these complicated feelings, they scolded and shamed her for wasting the money.

The critics were actually right, in a way. Jewish law said that care for the poor was an important part of religious life, especially around the time of Passover. Jesus also taught that care for the poor, sick, and imprisoned was the same as care for him (Matt. 25:31–46). He repeatedly encouraged the use of one's wealth for the poor (Luke 16:19–31; 18:18–25).

The critics also made a valid point about waste. Once the expensive oil was poured out and the beautiful scent dissipated into the air, there was nothing to show for the money she spent. How many poor people could have been fed? How many orphans housed?

In this situation, however, Jesus dismissed their complaints. "Let her alone; why do you trouble her? She has performed a good service for me. For you always have the poor with you, and you can show kindness to them whenever you wish; but you will not always have me. She has done what she could; she has anointed my body beforehand for its burial" (Mark 14:6–8).

Jesus saw her action as a beautiful act of love and affection ("a good service" in the NRSV is better translated as "a beautiful thing"). She chose to spend a great deal of money on this extravagant, seemingly wasteful gift, but she did not do it to draw attention to herself. It was a grand gesture that demonstrated how much she cared for him. Jesus did not second-guess the wisdom of her choice but responded to her great generosity with gratitude.

Jesus saw her affection for him, and he saw something else as well. Anointing with perfume was a ritual that women performed for dead bodies as a way to honor them and to cover the odor of decay. Her action anticipated his imminent death. Jesus had repeatedly told the disciples that he would die, but they refused to believe it. The woman understood, as the disciples did not, that Jesus' role as Messiah would include suffering and death. Jesus said she anointed him for his burial.

Her action had a third layer of significance. She anointed Jesus just as prophets had often anointed Israelite kings in the past. The prophet Samuel anointed David long before he became king of Israel (1 Sam. 16:13) because Samuel saw that David was called to something significant. Similarly, the woman perceived that Jesus was not an ordinary person but was called to something much bigger. She saw that he was the Messiah.

For all these reasons, Jesus affirmed the woman's action as appropriate, generous, and gracious. "She has done what she could" (Mark 14:8). She took what was available to her, this perfumed oil, and used it to make a grand gesture of love. She could not give a speech in the center of Jerusalem on behalf of Jesus. She could not prevent his death on the cross or take down his body once he was dead. But she could perform this act of love.

At the end of this encounter, Jesus made an extraordinary statement about this woman. "Wherever the good news is proclaimed in the whole world, what she has done will be told in remembrance of her" (Mark 14:9). Is this true? Have you ever heard a sermon about this story? Her action is recorded in this text, but her name is lost to us and her action has not been widely celebrated in the Christian tradition.

What is more often remembered about this story are these words of Jesus, "You always have the poor with you, and you can show kindness to them whenever you wish; but you will not always have me" (14:7). Jesus was referring to Jewish tradition, which saw the care of dead bodies as a significant religious responsibility. Bodies had to be cared for immediately at the time of death, because bodies decayed quickly in hot weather. Jesus was not callously dismissing the obligation to care for the poor, but acknowledging that while poverty may not be time-sensitive, poor people could and should be cared for at any time.

The woman is not named in Mark and Matthew's story,[1] but she is portrayed as an exemplary disciple, especially compared to the men who appear before and after her in the story. In Mark 14:1, the religious leaders are looking for a discreet way to have Jesus killed. The guests at the dinner fail to understand Jesus' mission and criticize the woman who does understand it. After the anointing, in 14:10–11, the disciple Judas offers to betray Jesus for money. The men are angry, vengeful, greedy, and selfish. This unnamed woman, on the other hand, demonstrates wisdom, awareness, and generosity. Her actions were a gift to Jesus. Her memory is a gift to us.

Diving Deeper

"You always have the poor with you." These words of Jesus have frequently been used to justify neglect of the poor. If poverty can never be alleviated, why try? Why spend money to help poor people when there will always be poor people? Is it better to make a grand gesture, as the woman did, to honor Jesus? While Christians can no longer pour expensive perfume on Jesus' head, they can certainly make a financial grand gesture of donating money to build a cathedral or a church ministry center or a college library or a community well in Africa.

When the Notre Dame Cathedral in Paris burned in April 2019, some donors immediately pledged one hundred million euros to rebuild. They were asked why they had never donated similar amounts to care for the poor. There will always be poor people, some responded, but there is only one Notre Dame. It is a symbol of Paris, and the millions of euros required to rebuild were considered money well spent.

This debate occurs in less dramatic fashion whenever a congregation considers a building program. Those in favor of a new addition argue that a functional and energy-efficient building with space for community outreach is a way to honor God, love Jesus, empower people, and care for the poor. It offers a place to encounter the holy in worship, connect with God's people, and find resources for service.

Critics of the building program might respond that buildings are expensive and require constant upkeep, and often a building designed to honor God in one generation (a sanctuary seating a thousand people, twenty classrooms, but no parking) is a millstone around the neck of the next generation. Better for church members to offer genuine care to the marginalized people in their communities, who are poor because of oppressive systems and not their lack of faith!

It is an exhausting and unsatisfying debate that becomes even more complicated when names are involved. If a new wing of the church, the library at the Christian college, or the gymnasium at the youth center is named for the largest donor, is that donation honoring God or the donor? It can do both, of course, but naming a building after the donor may make the grand gesture a little less grand.

What does it mean to be a disciple? How do we best show love for Jesus? If this woman is the model disciple who is praised for her action, should followers of Jesus go and do likewise? Contemporary Christians cannot show gratitude by pouring oil on his head, since Jesus is not here physically. But perhaps following Jesus means making a grand gesture of money, time, or self-sacrifice. Or does discipleship mean quietly following Jesus and showing generosity to the poor?

"She has done what she could." The Christian tradition has disagreed over the best way to honor Jesus. What if instead of fighting about what was best, we just did what we could? Living out and supporting the passion in your heart. Doing what fits with your abilities and resources, whether intellectual, spiritual, financial, or hospitable. Some may choose giving to the poor and others may choose the grand gesture. But there is room and need for all of it! If we were all this generous, if we all actually did what we could, the poor would be cared for and the local churches would be thriving.

What do you see? The guests at the dinner saw the woman's gift as extravagance and waste. They may have honestly been thinking about their responsibility to the poor, or they may have been selfish, cranky, and jealous. Either way, they assumed the worst of her and then tried to shame her. Jesus, on the other hand, saw honor, love, and devotion. Jesus told them not to bother her.

She saw more clearly than the disciples who Jesus was and what would happen to him. What do you see in other people? Potential? Giftedness? Generosity? What do you hope people see in you?

In memory of her. What will you be remembered for? Alfred Nobel, the inventor of dynamite and other explosives, did not want to be remembered for deadly creations. In his will, he left his large fortune to establish prizes for physics, chemistry, literature, and most significantly, peace.

If your obituary were written today, what would people remember about you? Is that the legacy you want to leave?

Questions for Reflection and Discussion

What does kindness to the poor look like? Charity? Systemic social change? Both? Something else?

How do you receive gifts? When someone is kind and gracious to you, do you dismiss their actions with "Oh, you shouldn't have"? Or can you receive graciously?

What does generosity look like? How do you express love and gratitude? Most of us do not have one hundred million euros or a year's salary to spend on perfumed oil. What does generosity look like when givers are not wealthy?

What makes us angry? The dinner guests were angry at the wrong thing!

A GRATEFUL WOMAN
(Luke 7)

The third season of the British television show *Downton Abbey* featured a story line about a housemaid named Ethel. She becomes pregnant during a relationship with a recuperating soldier during the war. The soldier dies, she loses her job, and she turns to prostitution to support herself and the baby. Two years later, Isobel Crawley, the do-gooder relative, hires Ethel as her housemaid. Isobel then invites the Crawley women to lunch. Mr. Carson, the butler, pompously fumes that a "woman of the streets" would be serving the women of the family. Robert Crawley, the father and husband, appears at the lunch and announces that he is escorting all the women home because Isobel and Ethel have exposed his family to scandal. His wife, Cora, refuses to leave, and instead compliments the cake Ethel has prepared. Robert again insists that the women leave, but his mother, Violet, the dowager countess, replies that it is a pity to leave such a good pudding (dessert). Robert slams the door as he leaves in disgust. Later in the episode, Mr. Carson is rude to Ethel when she brings flowers to thank the Downton cook for her help.[2]

Both men fear that the honor of the household and the virtue of the women can be corrupted by the presence of a former prostitute. They believe that scandal is contagious, like a disease. Even though Ethel now holds a "respectable" position as a maid, they think she is dirty and that her dirt could soil the Crawley family. The Crawley women, perhaps more aware of the realities of life, especially for vulnerable servant girls, do not fear being infected by Ethel's past.

Prostitution is known as the oldest profession, and even strict religious cultures have their share of prostitutes. Sex workers are criticized as dirty, dangerous, and immoral, but they continue to be hired. Their customers are rarely treated with the same disgust.

Moral judgments about prostitution have shifted in the last two decades as people have learned more about the sex-trafficking business and realized that many women have become trapped in prostitution and cannot escape. Traffickers promise young girls and their families that the girls will have jobs as nannies or food service workers, but the girls soon learn that their job is prostitution. Some women may "choose" prostitution because they have no other option to support themselves and their families. These women are often shamed and shunned.

The disgust for "fallen" women was even stronger in Jesus' time. In Luke 7, Jesus is invited to a dinner at the home of Simon the Pharisee. A woman interrupts the dinner, weeps profusely over Jesus' feet, dries them with her hair, and pours perfume on his feet. This is one of four stories in the Gospels in which a woman anoints Jesus at a dinner party. Luke is the only one who identifies her as "a sinner," so this version is a bit different from the others.

You may be picturing an awkward scene where men are sitting on chairs around a table, and the woman crawls under the table to reach the feet of Jesus. It is more likely that the guests were reclining on couches set around a central table. Their heads and hands were near the table with the food and their feet would have been at the outer end of the couch. The woman could easily reach Jesus' feet without crawling under the table.

It was customary at a dinner party that poor people were allowed to enter the home, sit along the side walls, and wait quietly to see if leftovers were available. It was *not* customary for a woman to approach a guest as this woman did.

The story does not say how the woman knew Jesus, but somehow he had made a difference in her life. She came to express her gratitude, perhaps thinking she could quietly anoint him and move on. But as she knelt at the end of Jesus' couch, she was overcome with emotion, perhaps a mix of love, regret, joy, shame, and loss. She could not stop crying, and her tears poured onto the feet of Jesus. This probably made her feel even more awkward and embarrassed, so she tried to dry his feet with her loosened hair. Finally she poured the expensive ointment on his feet.

This was a serious breach of etiquette.[3] Women were not supposed to touch men, let alone touch a man's feet in such an intimate way. Her actions were excessive, extravagant, and kind of weird. To make matters worse, she had a questionable reputation.

Simon and the other dinner guests wondered why Jesus allowed her to do this. Did Jesus know her? How could a good man allow a woman with a questionable reputation to touch him in such an intimate way? Why didn't he push her away? Tell her not to bother him?

The story describes her as "a sinner," and commentaries have often assumed that her sin was sexual. Commentators label the story with titles like "The Pharisee and the Harlot." They assume she was a prostitute, the "worst" kind of sinner, who sold her body for sex. Some commentators use the description "a woman in the city" to argue that she was a streetwalker. They point out that she had money for scented ointment, which they insist was a tool of the trade. Some commentators also note that a "good" woman would never loosen her hair, so she must be a prostitute.

The story does not use the typical Greek word for a prostitute, *pornē*. It calls her a *hamartōlos*, which was the standard word for "sinner." The disciple Peter identifies himself as a *hamartōlos* in Luke 5:8, and commentators never speculate that he was sexually immoral! A woman in that culture might be described as a *hamartōlos* if she had an illness or a disability, because both conditions were considered divine punishments for sinful behavior. She could be labeled sinful if she was a Jewish midwife who cared for Gentile women. She might have been married to a man who was considered a sinner. She might not have kept Jewish law strictly enough. She might have been the victim of rape or sexual abuse. She might have had a child before marriage.

Whatever the nature of her sin, Simon the Pharisee was offended by her presence. She did not belong at a dinner for respectable people. She brought shame. She threatened the reputation of the guests. Simon could not understand why Jesus was not equally offended by her presence. If Jesus was really a prophet with a gift of discernment, why didn't he realize that this woman was a sinner?

Jesus was indeed a prophet, and he used his prophetic gift to discern

Simon's snobbish and judgmental thoughts! Instead of confronting him directly, Jesus told Simon a story about forgiveness and gratitude. Two men owed a third man money. One owed about $5,000, the other $50,000. The creditor canceled both debts. Jesus asked who would be more grateful. Simon replied it would be the one who was forgiven more.

Jesus then observed that Simon had failed to carry out the traditional duties of a host. He had not provided water so that Jesus could wash his feet. He had not given the traditional kiss of greeting. He had not offered perfume, essential in a hot climate where people could not bathe very often. Then Jesus said pointedly to Simon, "Do you see this woman?" Do you see how loving she is? She did what Simon should have done. She washed, perfumed, and kissed him, not out of sexual impropriety, but out of love and gratitude. She loved much, Jesus said, because she had been forgiven much. Simon saw the woman as a sinner and rejected her. Jesus saw her as a grateful person and welcomed her. Simon had a vision problem.

The unspoken question that Jesus asked Simon was, "Do you see yourself?" And again, Simon had a vision problem. He saw the sin of the woman, but he did not see his own sin, his lack of hospitality, his sense of superiority. Instead, he saw himself as a good person who was devoted to his religion, who worked hard, who did what he was supposed to do. The righteous, priggish, well-behaved Simon did not feel any great need for forgiveness. And without experiencing forgiveness, he did not feel much gratitude.

I wonder if what Jesus offered the woman was not forgiveness so much as a release from the shame she felt as a broken or damaged or fallen woman in that culture. She might have been accustomed to men treating her as an object rather than a person. But Jesus saw her. He was not offended by her touch, even if it was unconventional. He did not view her actions as a kind of sexual come-on. He did not assume that she was trying to embarrass or humiliate him. He saw instead that she was grateful and caring. At some point in the past, the two of them might have had an encounter in which Jesus acknowledged and affirmed her as a person. He had made a difference in her life, and she had come to thank him. Jesus saw her action for what it was. Love. Gratitude.

Do you see this woman? She knew she was a sinner, and she knew she was forgiven. And that self-knowledge produced gratitude that could not be stopped by either the judgment of the rest of the dinner party or her embarrassment about her tears. She experienced God's grace so profoundly that it led her to an excessive, extravagant action that showed her love for Jesus.

Diving Deeper

What character do you identify with in this story? Were you the model child in your family who excelled in school and sports and did everything right? Or were you the rebellious one who pushed the limits and acted out and made decisions you regretted? Are you an upright guy like Simon? Or do you have a reputation you are not particularly proud of? Or do you see yourself as a person who has made mistakes but has been forgiven and graced with a new start? It might be more difficult for the successful Simons to realize their need of healing and forgiveness, because they've been generally well behaved.

Reduced to tears? What makes you cry? We often use the phrase "reduced to tears," but I wonder if we actually cry when we are full. Full of joy, sorrow, anger, humiliation, longing, grief, or gratitude. The provost at my college teared up when giving her first speech to the faculty. This can be embarrassing for women leaders who would rather not hear that they are "too emotional." She did not apologize but simply said, "Can you tell I care about this?"

Sometimes we cry in church. When we sing a hymn like "Gather Us In" I feel profoundly grateful for a worshiping community that is genuinely inclusive of all God's people. But I have also cried out of frustration, often at denominational meetings, when my denomination has been profoundly unwelcoming in its language or policies or decisions. We cry about things that matter, and that is nothing to be embarrassed about.

Forgiven. Sometimes the church and religious people speak of forgiveness in a way that emphasizes how terrible the forgiven people were and still are. Jesus has sacrificed his life in order to forgive them for being awful people. They should be ashamed of themselves and always remember they are unworthy. Ruth Everhart describes an incident that occurred when she was about seven. She had to meet with the pastor of her church, who asked why she loved Jesus. She said, "Because he first loved me." The minister said she was right, but then jabbed his index finger into her palm and said, "He loved you so much He had *nails* driven into His hands for you. Without Him, you are nothing, do you hear me? Nothing!"[4]

Thankfully, Jesus did not operate this way! Jesus saw people in need of forgiveness and healing and a new start. But they were never nothing to him. They were always people of worth, whom he valued and respected. People did not need to be completely torn down and built up again. Their gifts, their interests, their personalities needed to be healed and transformed.[5]

Do you see? Simon saw the woman as a sinner. Jesus saw her as a person. Do you see people? What do you see when you walk by a group of homeless people? When you see a group of undocumented immigrants on the news? Are they undesirables? Criminals? Failures? Or beloved children of God?

It may be even more difficult to see and acknowledge those people we disagree with. Nadia Bolz-Weber is a Lutheran pastor who recently wrote a book about sexuality in the Christian tradition. She interviewed members of her congregation who had at times been judged and shamed for their sexual orientation or gender identity. She criticized pastors and authors who damaged people with their judgmental words. And yet, she writes that God asks her to see them too.

> Are they complex, hurting, wonderfully made children of God with whom I deeply disagree, or are they only as I want to see them—sinners? . . . Even if it is the last thing I want to do, I absolutely have to believe the Gospel is powerful enough, transgressive enough, beautiful enough to heal not only the ones who have been hurt but also those who have done the hurting.
>
> Do we *see* them? Do we see the ways in which they were in all likelihood trying to be faithful? Do we see the ways in which we, too, may have inadvertently, in our own desire to be faithful, hurt others?[6]

When have you felt most loved and accepted? Imagine that you are in the grocery store and one of your children has a meltdown in frozen foods. A full-scale, lie-on-the-floor-kicking-and-screaming tantrum. One person passes by and rolls her eyes in disgust, pronouncing you a terrible mother. Another woman comes by and smiles sympathetically. She makes a little joke about toddler oppositional defiant disorder and asks if there is anything she can do to help. Maybe she helps you pick up the rigid child and corral the rest of the kids and your cart to a quieter place where you can all regroup. Which one of those people is going to make you feel slightly less terrible about your parenting skills at that moment? The first woman demonstrates judgment. She adds to the shame you are already feeling as an inadequate parent. The second woman demonstrates empathy. She has been here. She acknowledges with her presence and concern and smile that you are a perfectly adequate parent currently in the grip of a very annoying toddler.

How many people in the world need to be seen and acknowledged and affirmed? Some people are perhaps more sinned against than sinful. Victims of violence. People who have been punished for being gay or lesbian or transgender. People who had emotionally abusive parents. Kids with learning disabilities who were shamed for being stupid. People with social anxieties. These people don't need forgiveness so much as they need someone in their life to say, I see you. I see how hard it was. I see how you felt put down or betrayed or violated. I see the pain. It wasn't your fault.

When we experience that kind of acceptance, affirmation, and empathy from God or another person, whether in church or school or the workplace, whether we are nine or nineteen or ninety, we might be not reduced to tears but overflowing with them. Like the woman in Luke 7, hopefully we will be grateful. And we can take the radical affirmation, the feeling that comes from being seen, and we can use it to see others.

Grateful. In her memoir *A Fighting Chance,* Senator Elizabeth Warren often returns to the theme of gratitude. She describes a time in her childhood when her father had lost his job and her stay-at-home mother with no work experience had to find a job to keep the family afloat. She celebrates the family members who came to live with her when she was having a hard time meeting the combined demands of law school and parenting. She appreciates the people who told her what it meant to lose their homes in the financial crisis. She praises the people who worked so hard in her Senate campaign. She realizes that while she has worked hard her entire life, she has also been helped at every stage by other people. And she is grateful to them. She knows she did not succeed alone.[7]

A genuine expression of gratitude does not require a grand gesture, tears, and expensive ointment. Most of the time, a simple acknowledgment that someone helped you is a meaningful way to say thank you.

Questions for Reflection and Discussion

Who do you eat with? It still matters, especially in middle school! If you sit with the wrong person, your status can go down.

Is there a difference between healing and forgiveness?

Have you ever had a bout of uncontrollable crying? What caused it?

When have you felt seen and known and cared for? When have you felt shamed and worthless?

What does it mean to see the people who are hurting other people? Misusing their power? How much of that mean-spirited behavior is rooted in their own struggles with shame, anxiety, and the sense of not being good enough?

What and whom do you need to see more clearly?

5

The Sisters

MARY AND MARTHA, PART 1
(Luke 10:38–42)

Sisterhood is complicated! Sisters can be best friends or constant competitors or both. They may have each other's back or be willing to stab each other in the back. They have a long history and know each other's vulnerabilities. They share memories, joys, and sorrows.

The New Testament says little about siblings, which may be why the stories about Mary and Martha are so intriguing. The siblings Mary and Martha and Lazarus were close friends of Jesus. The Gospels tell three stories about them. In Luke 10, Jesus comes to dinner at the home of Mary and Martha. In John 11, Lazarus dies and Jesus raises him from the dead. In John 12, Jesus attends a dinner at the home of Lazarus. Martha serves the meal, and Mary pours perfume on Jesus' feet.

The first story appears in Luke. Jesus, likely accompanied by the disciples, came to Martha's home for dinner. Martha was busy preparing the meal while her sister Mary sat at the feet of Jesus, listening to him teach. Martha resented being left with all the work, and she complained to Jesus and suggested that he tell Mary to help her in the kitchen. Jesus gently chastised Martha for being too anxious about the kitchen work and said that Mary had chosen the "better part" (Luke 10:42).

This story has sparked a lot of discussion and controversy. Is Jesus criticizing Martha? If so, what does this mean for all the service work women have been doing in the church? Are all the church women's groups doing the wrong things?

How would churches survive without their Marthas?

When a funeral is held in my congregation, a group of women assemble the ham-on-buns (a Midwestern staple), set the tables, clear the tables, and wash the dishes. Often they sit at the end of the buffet line pouring tea and coffee from elegant silver pots, which adds a touch of grace to a sad occasion.

Other women regularly provide meals to members of the congregation who are ill or give birth or need encouragement. Some women cross-stitch baptismal banners. Some tend the infants in the nursery. Some assemble the newsletter.

Men can be Marthas too. Some of them cook, teach, and organize, but they might also shovel snow from the front steps, mow the church lawn, tend the gardens, or fix the stubborn boiler.

Marthas are everywhere in congregations; they are the men and women who are responsible for much of congregational life. The ham sandwiches do not miraculously appear on the tables for the funeral lunch. The coffeepot does not start itself on Sunday morning. A potluck might spread out the cooking responsibilities, but somebody has to wash the silverware. Salt does not fall on the icy sidewalk like manna from heaven. A can of Campbell's chicken soup does not say love quite like the homemade version brought by one of the church ladies. So much care and compassion have been shown to church members and friends by Martha and her friends.

So when Jesus chastises Martha for being too anxious about the meal, we might take offense! Jesus might have arrived unannounced with twelve hungry disciples, and perhaps Martha was trying to figure out how to stretch a pound of hamburger meant for three into a meal for sixteen. It takes a lot of work to cook for a group and have everything ready at the right time. Martha might have been a little stressed, and she might have hoped that somebody would volunteer to chop the vegetables or stir the soup. It was not likely to be one of the disciples, so Mary was probably her only source of assistance. We can't judge Martha too harshly for asking for some help. But Jesus told her that she was too fussy and anxious and should not force Mary out of her position as a learner and into the kitchen. Does Jesus seem a little insensitive here? After all, dinner is not going to fix itself!

If Martha was doing what women usually did (in that culture and most cultures since then), Mary was doing something that women usually did not do. She was learning about religion. She had chosen the traditional student's position at the feet of the teacher to listen to Jesus. Women were not supposed to do that. Some religious scholars thought women were unable to learn religious material because they lacked the intellect to grasp it. Some thought it was inappropriate to allow weak and unclean women to learn holy things. Others considered it a waste of time to teach religious material to women, who should focus their energies on cooking, cleaning, and child care. Any woman who wanted to learn was thought to be stepping out of her appropriate place and perhaps also seeking inappropriate relationships with men.

In affirming Mary's choice to learn, Jesus did something radical. He said that she had the capacity to learn and that it was proper for her to do so. It was not offensive or foolish or a waste of time to teach women the laws and the stories of the faith. Mary was not stepping out of her place. She was a disciple, a learner, a follower of Jesus, just like the male disciples.

Jesus told Martha that Mary had chosen wisely, even though her choice to learn was not typical for women of that time. Martha needed to recognize that Mary's desire to study was valid and important. Jesus refused to sacrifice Mary's interest in learning to the social expectation that she do domestic work.

Too often women's education has been curtailed so that they can do housework or get a job to support the family. John Calvin and other Protestant Reformers thought that girls should be taught to read so that they could read the Bible, a progressive view for the time, but did not encourage formal education for girls as they did for boys. In the early nineteenth century, many young women worked in the textile industry for long hours and low pay so that their brothers could go to college. They did not have the opportunity to go to college themselves.

Jesus did not criticize Martha so much as remind her that she need not be consumed by anxiety over her domestic responsibilities. He probably appreciated a good meal, but he may have been gently saying that bread and cheese and wine would have been enough. A simple supper would have allowed Martha to listen and learn also. Her choice to cook was not wrong, or even inappropriate, but he was trying to free her from the societal expectation that no respectable woman fixes Kraft macaroni and cheese for guests.

Martha felt bound by social expectations to perform in a particular way, and she demanded that her sister live up to the same expectations.

Women cooked. Mary was a woman. Therefore Mary should help with the cooking. That was the way things worked in their world. But Jesus said no. Martha could choose to care for Jesus by cooking, but she could not force Mary to make the same choice. If Mary wanted to learn, she should not be forced into the kitchen.

Jesus' words offered women the freedom to study and learn, but over time the actions of Mary were reinterpreted and used to restrict women. Before the nineteenth century, most Roman Catholic women who entered the convent spent their time in prayer, contemplation, and worship. They were told to imitate Mary and quietly and passively devote themselves to God. When some orders of nuns saw the great needs in the world for education and health care, and tried to serve as teachers and nurses, they were told that such work was too worldly and therefore inappropriate for them. After all, Jesus told Martha that Mary had chosen the better part! Nevertheless, these nuns persisted! Women religious have started hospitals (including the Mayo Clinic) and schools and mission programs and social service agencies. They have made an extraordinary difference in the world, but they had to fight for the right to do so.

In the last two centuries, Protestant and Catholic women have been allowed and encouraged to do the Martha work that keeps a church alive and engaged with the world. They were not always encouraged to engage in the theological education that would enable them to become pastors and leaders in the church.

That has changed dramatically in the last fifty years, and women now comprise the majority of students at many seminaries. Women are now pastors in most mainline denominations. At times there has been tension between the women called to official church leadership and those who are not. At times, especially in the early years of women's ordination, the Marthas, who had done the cooking and cleaning for years, resented the Marys who now held positions as pastors and teachers. Some of the Marys have not always valued the work of the Marthas. There were painful conflicts and misunderstandings. But God calls and gifts everyone in various ways. Not every woman is cut out for seminary or leadership. Neither is every man. "There are varieties of gifts, but the same Spirit" (1 Cor. 12:4).

Thank God for the Marthas who do so much to keep the church alive and vibrant! And thank God for the Marys who are called to study, prayer, presence, or preaching. Both callings are important. Neither Marthas nor Marys should expect or force others to do as they do.

The kinds of service and discipleship we engage in depend on gifts and inclinations, not gender roles.

What if Jesus and the disciples and Mary had all helped Martha prepare the meal and clean up, and then they had all sat around talking afterward!

Diving Deeper

She has stepped out of her place. In 1635, Anne Hutchinson (1591– 1643) arrived in Boston with her family. She had received a theological education from her father, an Anglican minister. She began offering women's Bible studies in which she explained the Sunday sermon in a way that people found more accessible than the sermons themselves. Men began attending as well, and the Puritan leaders got nervous about a woman teaching men. They asked who gave her the authority, and she said that the Holy Spirit spoke to her directly! She was brought to trial and eventually excommunicated from the church and banished from the community. The men in charge pronounced that her crime was that she had stepped out of her place and taken on a man's role.

Peg was one of the first women to be elected an elder (lay leader) in a Reformed Church congregation in the 1970s. At her first meeting of the consistory (leadership group), the members enjoyed blueberry pie. Peg joked that she hoped the pie had not turned her teeth blue. One of the male elders advised that she just keep her mouth shut.

Unfortunately, there are countless ways in which women have not been supported in their desire to learn and lead. Instead, they have been silenced and shamed, but they have learned to live with resistance and to resist themselves.

Yearning for learning. Denying women a formal education does not end their desire to learn. In the movie *Yentl*, set in Poland around 1900, a young Jewish woman studies religious teachings with her father, a rabbi. When he dies, she tries to pursue formal Jewish education, but it is prohibited for women. She dresses as a man and goes to school, where she excels and thrives, until complications in life and love force her to reveal her gender.

Sarah Grimké (1792–1873) read her brother's textbooks because she was eager to learn but not permitted to go to college. Her father said that Sarah would have made a good judge, but of course that was not an option for her in the 1820s. She became an abolitionist and an early advocate for women's rights.

Roles are rules. As a child, teen, and adult in the church, were you taught that there were particular roles for men and women? How were those rules conveyed to you? What was the "punishment" for challenging the rules? Did your gifts fit with the expectations? Did you rebel?

What about now? Do you ever get tired of your role in the church? Do you wish you could try something different and get out of the kitchen? Do you think there is a hierarchy of gifts? Are preachers and leaders more valued than Sunday school teachers? Is that legitimate? Fair?

Questions for Reflection and Discussion

Why did Jesus say Mary chose the better part?

What are examples of Mary's and Martha's gifts? How does each serve the church? Follow Jesus?

What does it mean to be a disciple?

Have you ever observed or experienced resentment between the Marys and the Marthas in the church? Why might that exist? How might it be healed?

MARY AND MARTHA, PART 2
(John 11–12)

The other two stories involving Mary and Martha are quite different. The sisters are not in conflict in these stories, but are united in their grief over a loss and in their love for Jesus.

Mary and Martha have a brother named Lazarus, who is very ill, and they send word to inform Jesus. They do not explicitly ask him to come, but seem to expect that he will do something. Jesus does nothing! He tells the disciples that Lazarus's illness will lead not to his death, but to God's glory. Several days later, Jesus and the disciples finally visit the family, but by then Lazarus has been dead for four days.

When Martha hears that Jesus is coming, she goes out to meet him and says, "Lord, if you had been here, my brother would not have died. But even now I know that God will give you whatever you ask of him" (John 11:21). Consider the depth of pain and grief in that statement. Her brother is dead. She has seen Jesus' healing powers and knows that he could have saved Lazarus. But Jesus did not come and did not heal Lazarus from afar. She must have felt a powerful sense of loss and confusion. If Jesus cared about them, why didn't he heal Lazarus? Did Jesus not care? Or did he lack the power to heal?

Contemporary readers understand these questions and Martha's resentment. It is not clear why God heals sometimes and not others. Are we not good enough? Did we not pray enough? Did God have a mysterious plan? Was it God's will that someone die? If God is good and yet doesn't heal, does God lack the power to do so? Or does God possess the power but choose not to use it?

Jesus tells Martha that her brother will rise again. She believes this, but assumes he will rise in the future. "I know that he will rise again in the resurrection on the last day." Jesus says to her, "I am the resurrection and the life. Those who believe in me, even though they die, will live. . . . Do you believe this?" (John 11:24–26).

Martha responds with one of the most powerful and theologically astute faith statements in the Gospels: "Yes, Lord, I believe that you are the Messiah, the Son of God, the one coming into the world" (11:27).

Her words are very similar to Peter's confession in Matthew 16:16, "You are the Messiah, the Son of the living God." Jesus praises Peter for his faith and promises that he will be a key player in the early church. Martha's comment shows a similar degree of faith, trust, and insight into Jesus' identity, yet some commentators ignore that. Instead, they criticize Martha for her presumption in asking Jesus to heal Lazarus in the first place, for "guilting" Jesus for his absence, and for seeming to manipulate Jesus when she says that God will give him whatever he asks.

After this conversation, Martha returns home and tells her sister Mary that she has seen Jesus, so Mary also goes to him, along with a number of fellow mourners. She kneels at his feet and says the same words that Martha had said. "Lord, if you had been here, my brother would not have died" (John 11:32). She shows confidence in him, but it is also a gentle reproach, because Jesus had not been there.

Jesus sees Mary crying, and the mourners crying, and he is angry and upset. His anger is confusing. Was he angry at a lack of faith in Mary and the mourners? Probably not, because Jesus also weeps, and the mourners conclude that his tears are a sign of deep love. Perhaps he is sad and frustrated about the continuing reality of death, which he cannot fully eradicate despite occasional healings. Perhaps he empathizes with the grief of others. Perhaps he feels his own grief at the loss of a friend, perhaps compounded by the fact that he did not heal Lazarus.

Jesus weeps, as they all do, out of love and loss and grief. Jesus does not tell them that Lazarus is in a better place, or that God needed him more than they did. He does not tell them that big girls don't cry. He does not shame them for their grief or tell them to stop crying. Instead, he cries with them. He knows that the pain of loss is real and needs to be expressed rather than stifled or dismissed. He is not "reduced" to tears; he cries because his heart is full.

It is striking that Mary and Martha both speak freely to Jesus about their grief and loss and disappointment. "If you had been here . . ." They are not afraid of him. They do not need to sugarcoat the truth to spare his feelings. They are hurting, and they express that via lament. They are not passive, subservient disciples who must keep their opinions to themselves. They are adult friends of Jesus[1] and they can tell him what they think without fearing that they might offend him or hurt his feelings. Martha does the same in Luke 10:40 when she tells Jesus what to do about her slacker sister! Jesus listens and takes them seriously.

Jesus does not offer excuses for his absence. He goes to the tomb and orders that the stone be rolled away. Martha reminds him that after four days, the unembalmed body will have decayed in the heat and it will smell. But Jesus commands Lazarus to come out of the tomb, and he does! There is much rejoicing because the dead man has been raised.

Mary anoints Jesus. In this story (John 12:1–8), Lazarus hosts a dinner for Jesus, perhaps in gratitude for raising him from the dead. Martha serves. Mary anoints Jesus' head with expensive perfume. If this action sounds familiar, it is because you have read two versions of it already in this book. In the Gospels of Matthew and Mark, an unnamed woman anoints Jesus' head with oil to honor him before his death. In the Gospel of Luke, an unnamed woman labeled as sinful washes Jesus' feet with her tears, dries them with her hair, and anoints them with scented ointment.

This story draws elements from the other two stories. Mary of Bethany is identified as the anointer in this story, while the other three women are unnamed. The dinner party occurs during the week of Passover, and Mary is said to be anointing Jesus for burial, as are the women in Mark and Matthew. Those women anoint Jesus' head, but Mary anoints his feet, like the "sinful" woman. John Calvin tried to harmonize the stories by insisting that Mary poured the oil on his head but it ran down to his feet. If Jesus was lying stretched out on a couch, that is particularly unlikely!

In all four stories, one or more of the men at the dinner complain about her action, either because she was sinful (Luke), or because she wasted money that should have been given to the poor. John identifies Judas Iscariot as the critic, and notes that he was about to betray Jesus and that he had a habit of stealing the money from the common purse. Jesus makes the same response to Judas that he did in Mark and Matthew. "Leave her alone. She bought it so that she might keep it for the day of my burial. You always have the poor with you, but you do not always have me" (John 12:8).

Like the women in the Mark and Matthew stories, Mary of Bethany is making a grand gesture. She crashed a dinner party where women may have been welcome as servers but probably not as guests. Her brother may have been hosting and her sister serving, but her action would still have been seen as strange and invasive. She brought expensive oil, worth a year's wages. She poured it on his feet, and the aroma filled the room. She may have realized that the oil was slippery and messy, so she wiped his feet with her long loose hair. Loose hair was considered inappropriate in a public place, because it was a sign of intimacy that should be saved for one's husband.

Why his feet? Pouring oil on Jesus' head seems strange enough, but kneeling over someone's dusty, dirty, smelly feet seems like a particularly humiliating and degrading gesture. But she did it as an act of love.

There is a larger significance to her action. She discerns the future and intuits that death is coming for Jesus. She cannot do anything to stop the political and religious machine from rolling on and destroying him. But she can care for him now in this humble and intimate way. Anointing his feet was a way to show respect, love, and honor. She did not ask permission. She decided for herself how to minister to Jesus.

Her action connects to the following chapter (John 13), in which Jesus takes a towel and washes the feet of the disciples. The Greek word used for wiping his feet with her hair is the same word used when Jesus wipes the feet of the disciples with a towel. Both Mary and Jesus model true discipleship and service and care for others. Mary has done for him what he will do for the disciples and what he will ask them to do for each other.

Mary's grand gesture gets all the attention, while Martha's care for Jesus is matter-of-factly reported in two words: "Martha served" (12:2). Cooking and serving is just what women do and often isn't acknowledged at all. The word for service is *diakonia*, which will be discussed in the chapter on Paul's letters. In the New Testament, the word has multiple meanings ranging from serving at table, to the more structured care of the poor in Acts, to the actions of ministers of the gospel. This suggests that Martha, in preparing and serving a meal, ministered to Jesus just as Mary did with her grand gesture.

In the Luke story, Mary sat quietly listening to Jesus so that she could learn from him. In this story she is acting on her faith and the knowledge she may have gained. Sometimes faith and discipleship are about sitting quietly and being instructed. Sometimes faith and discipleship are active: making a meal, anointing with perfume, speaking out, teaching, preaching. Some of us may be called to one style more than the other, but it's always a balance. The activists need to take some time to be nurtured and fed. Those who pray and study sometimes need to put words or legs to their prayers and engage in action.

Both women are disciples. They follow Jesus. They understand that he will be killed and are trying to care for him in advance. They understand that following Jesus will lead not to power and influence but to suffering and struggle.

Diving Deeper

"Lord, if you had been here." Mary and Martha are not shy about lamenting the loss of their brother and suggesting to Jesus that he had let them down. "Lord, if you had been here, my brother would not have died" (John 11:21, 32). Were the women wrong to say this? Were they too critical of Jesus? Or was this reaction part of their deep sense of loss? Similarly, is it appropriate to express frustration and even anger that people are not healed?

How do we deal with grief? It's OK to be sad, and it can take a very long time to process grief. It is highly unlikely that we will see a dead person being raised. How else might glimmers of new life begin to happen in our lives?

My friend Phil had outlived two wives by the time he reached eighty-five. He said he was done with relationships, because it was too painful to experience that kind of loss. Not long after, he befriended a woman who needed his care and companionship. He grew to love her and her family. After she died, he continued a close relationship with her daughter. Now that he is ninety, he occasionally says that he does not know why he is still around. But he always finds meaningful things to do. He wrote his memoirs, he traveled, he taught his native language, and most recently, he got rid of excess stuff so that his children will have less to do when he dies. Over and over, he has found a new sense of purpose and meaning in his life. That is one way that resurrection happens.

Louise had two much-loved older dogs that she regularly walked in the woods. One day one of them was stolen. Louise went to the woods every day to search for the stolen dog, and one day found a puppy that was sick, starving, and covered with ticks. Louise took her in, nursed her back to health, and now enjoys this new member of her family while still grieving her lost dog.

New life comes in many forms, from significant healing to new relationships to new pets. The grace and love of Jesus can heal our losses, help us find meaning in life, help us work through grief, and help us find joy in the memories of a person who has died.

She served. For centuries the church has assumed that women will cheerfully do the humble, behind-the-scenes work of food preparation and delivery and cleaning up. They will sew and clean and wash and care for the children. Life could not happen without these tasks, and yet men have often simply assumed that their meals will be provided, their clothes washed, their children tended.

When Mary served in a different, more dramatic and public way, she was criticized. The men tried to decide for her what was appropriate. Women should not be too passionate. They should not call attention to themselves. They should not be "too much." Better to stay in the background and cook, like Martha. There is a long history of men telling women what to do and how to behave. Jesus had no patience for this! He affirmed Mary and criticized Judas for judging her. And then Jesus took his cue from her and washed the disciples' feet.

Jesus models the humble service that we often connect with "women's work." And he instructs his disciples that they are called not to greatness or acclaim or wealth or power, but to service. At the same time, he elevates women and says that they are not bound to positions of menial service. That is the trouble with Jesus. He turns everything upside down. To those who would like a taste of power, he models servanthood. To those who have been serving all their lives, he offers an invitation to learn and to evangelize, and he praises their theological insight. Martha the servant sees that Jesus is the Messiah! Mary the servant sees that Jesus will be crucified. These two humble women are wise and insightful. Meanwhile the disciples, who would like to be powerful and in control and recognized, are told to wash each other's feet, as Jesus washed theirs.

How are followers of Jesus to sort out these instructions now? Do women need to be told to serve more than they already do? Or do they need to be encouraged to study and lead? Do men need to take their turn in the kitchen? The nursery? What do service and discipleship and following Jesus look like?

Questions for Reflection and Discussion

Can you envision yourself having an adult friendship with Jesus?

What are some of the ways you have experienced resurrection and new life?

What does it mean to be a disciple?

6

The Cross and the Empty Tomb

THE WOMEN PRESENT WITH JESUS
(Matthew 26–28*)

In this study of the women in the New Testament, we have explored about a dozen women who encountered Jesus during his lifetime on earth. If Jesus had three active years of ministry, that number seems low, although he probably met other women whose stories were not recorded. At the end of his life, a number of women appear at the cross and the resurrection. They rarely speak, many are unnamed, and their action usually consists of watching and waiting. But they are consistently, quietly present, and they play a significant role in witnessing and proclaiming the resurrection of Jesus. They were there all along.

Matthew, Mark, and Luke each devote three lengthy chapters to the death and resurrection of Jesus, while John uses nine. Each Gospel includes some different details, but the main outline of the story is similar. The authors describe the Last Supper, Jesus' prayers in the Garden of Gethsemane, his betrayal by Judas, his political and religious court hearings, the physical abuse he received, and finally the painful hours on the cross. Sadly, Jesus is often alone. He prays alone, because the disciples cannot stay awake. He is taken from one court to another,

---

* The story of the women present with Jesus also appears in Mark 14–16; Luke 22–24, John 13–21.

surrounded by accusers, not by friends. Peter denies that he knows Jesus. The disciples run away because they are afraid.

It was a dangerous time for the disciples, because followers and friends of a convicted criminal could be charged with similar crimes and given similar punishments. The disciples were operating on adrenaline and pure terror, and their instinct for self-preservation won out. In the end, the disciples failed as followers and friends. Their loyalty was tested and found wanting. They were more interested in saving their own skin than in being present with their leader in his suffering.

Each of the four Gospels contains a sentence like this one: "Many women were also there, looking on from a distance; they had followed Jesus from Galilee and had provided for him" (Matt. 27:55–56; see also Mark 15:40–41; Luke 23:49; John 19:25). This group of women had gathered around Jesus earlier in his ministry (Luke 8:2–3). Luke identifies three by name, Mary Magdalene, Joanna, and Susanna, and notes that there were "many others." Some had been healed by Jesus. Others wanted to follow and learn. These women traveled with Jesus and the disciples, providing financial resources and serving, which probably meant preparing meals and finding water. They accompanied Jesus on his final journey from Galilee to Jerusalem, a distance of about eighty miles, and they were present through the events of what we call Holy Week. The women had been present with Jesus throughout his ministry, and now they were at the cross.

The women remained at a distance, probably feeling frightened and powerless. They could not stand up to Pontius Pilate and demand he release Jesus. They could not confront the religious and political leaders who lied about Jesus. They could not speak in his defense. They could not protect their friend and teacher from the gruesome death to come. But they could be present. They could stay and watch. They did what they could.

Crucifixion was a long, brutal process of execution, and death usually resulted from suffocation. Consider how difficult it would have been for them to watch Jesus suffer such physical and psychological pain. Many people say it would be easier to feel the pain themselves than to watch someone they love in such anguish. Like the disciples, the women may have been tempted to flee to save themselves from grief. But they stayed. They watched. They waited.

When the ordeal was finally finished and Jesus had died, the women waited to see what would happen next. It was almost sundown on the day before the Jewish Sabbath, when no work could be done, so the body had to be cared for immediately. Joseph of Arimathea arranged to take the body of Jesus and put it in a tomb. The women followed along, watching. They were taking a risk in going to the tomb, but they wanted to see where Jesus was buried. They watched as his battered body was placed in a large space cut into rock, with another large, heavy rock to cover the opening.

The women went home and rested for a day, according to the rules of the Jewish Sabbath, but early the next morning, on Sunday, they went out, bought spices, and took them to the tomb. They would honor Jesus by sprinkling spices and perfume near his body. But there was no body! In each Gospel, the women are shocked to find that the tomb is empty. They had seen him die on the cross. They had seen his body placed in the tomb. What happened? Did someone steal his body? It made no sense.

Each of the four Gospels tells the Easter story a bit differently.[1] They share some common elements, such as unusual visitors at the tomb, but some distinct differences, such as the number and description of the visitors. In each story, women come to the tomb, but the number and identities of the women vary. The specific events also vary in each Gospel.

These differences in the resurrection accounts are not immediately obvious to people gathered in worship on Easter Sunday. The preacher probably chooses one Gospel story to read and discuss. The next year, the preacher might choose a different story, and most worshipers will not remember the details and differences. A careful comparison of the stories shows that each author tailored the stories for a different audience. The authors may have also used different sources that had relied on different memories. The early church might have dealt with these awkward contradictions by including only one Gospel in the New Testament, but instead the multiple perspectives were accepted and valued.

The authors knew that the resurrection was strange, unexpected, and difficult to explain, both at the time it occurred and many decades later. They were interested in the details, but even more, they considered the "so what" questions. What did the resurrection of Jesus mean for their lives? What did it mean for the early church? Two thousand years later, readers also wonder what the resurrection means for those who follow Jesus now.

To illustrate the differences in each story, here is a brief overview of each Gospel's description of the women at the tomb. This may seem a bit technical and even picky, but rather than try to create one big story that includes all the different details, it is more helpful to see each story on its own terms.

Mark 16. Mark's Gospel reports that Mary Magdalene, Salome, and

Mary the mother of James came to the tomb with spices. They wondered who would roll away the heavy stone that blocked the opening of the tomb, but when they arrived, the large stone had already been rolled away. They entered the tomb and saw a young man, dressed in white, who told them not to be afraid. He knew they were looking for Jesus of Nazareth. The young man said, "He has been raised; he is not here. Look, there is the place they laid him." The man then instructed them to tell the disciples and Peter that Jesus was going ahead to Galilee, and they would see him there, as Jesus had told them. The women were caught completely off guard by this strange, unexpected, unbelievable news. Jesus was dead. How could a dead man come to life? Mark reports, "So they went out and fled from the tomb, for terror and amazement had seized them; and they said nothing to anyone, for they were afraid" (16:8).

Was this the ending you expected? Where is the happy ending? Where is the resurrected Jesus? Where are the happy disciples? The women hear good news, but they are terrified.

Most New Testament scholars agree that Mark's version of the Gospel ends here at verse 8. The oldest manuscripts stop at verse 8. Your Bible probably includes some extra material, possibly enclosed in brackets. These verses, a shorter and a longer ending, are found only in later manuscripts of Mark's Gospel. Scholars have analyzed the language and content of both additional endings and concluded they are not original to Mark.[2] They were probably added to the Gospel by someone who thought that Mark's original ending was too dark and depressing and failed to adequately convey the good news of the resurrection.

Mark's original ending *is* dark and depressing, and it is not surprising that someone would have wanted to add a happier ending. Why would Mark have stopped where he did? Did the last page of the Gospel get lost somehow?

Mark may have heard a version of the Easter story that ended with the women's fear. When the author wrote down the story decades after it happened, he and his audience knew the whole story. Jesus had indeed been raised. The woman told the disciples and Jesus appeared to them. The early church developed on the basis of this good news. Mark may not have thought he needed to say this, since it was already known.

One commentator offers a helpful analogy. Imagine a video clip showing President John F. Kennedy and his wife, Jackie, riding in a convertible on the streets of Dallas in November 1963, smiling and waving to the crowd. The video ends on this happy note. Most adults older than fifty who see this clip will know exactly what happened moments later. JFK was shot, Mrs. Kennedy held his head in her lap, and there was mass confusion. Similarly, the author of Mark's Gospel may have assumed that he did not need to tell the whole story of the resurrection, because his readers knew how the story ended.[3]

Mark may also be making a theological point here. The disciples had repeatedly failed Jesus in his life and at his death. They were constantly confused about his mission and their part in it, no matter how often he explained. At the end of his life, they ran away in fear. The women were faithful at the cross, but they also ran away in fear when they saw the empty tomb. When Mark wrote this Gospel forty years later, he knew that the good news *did* get proclaimed. The women *did* go and tell the disciples. The power of God to bring about new life could not be permanently limited by human fear, sin, or uncertainty. God uses fallible humans to do much of God's work, but when they fail, God has a plan B.

Mark was writing at a time when Christians were being persecuted, and some of his readers may have failed at faithfulness. Mark's version of the Easter story would have reminded them that the good news was stronger than their failures. Fear might get the best of them at times, but there will always be an opportunity to tell the story again and choose a more courageous course of action.

Matthew 28. The Gospel of Matthew builds on Mark's version, adding dramatic details. Two women, Mary Magdalene and "the other Mary," approached the tomb. "Suddenly there was a great earthquake; for an angel of the Lord, descending from heaven, came and rolled back the stone and sat on it. His appearance was like lightning, and his clothing white as snow" (28:2–3). This was so terrifying that the guards assigned to monitor the tomb passed out from shock and fear. The angel reassured the women. "Do not be afraid; I know that you are looking for Jesus who was crucified. He is not here; for he has been raised, as he said" (vv. 5–6). As in Mark, the angel encouraged them to look into the tomb and see that Jesus was not there. Then the angel commissioned the women to go and tell the disciples that Jesus had risen and was going ahead to Galilee, where they would see him. The women "left the tomb quickly, with fear *and* great joy, and ran to tell his disciples" (v. 8, emphasis added). They hadn't gone far before Jesus himself showed up! They worshiped him, and Jesus sent them on their way to tell the disciples.

Matthew acknowledges that fear was the first response to these strange events. An earthquake! An angel! A missing body! Big strong soldiers fainting in fear! Both the angel and Jesus tell the women not to be afraid, and they leave the tomb to tell the disciples what they have seen. They joyfully greet Jesus when he meets them on the way. Here is the happy ending!

Luke 24. Luke begins his resurrection account by saying that "they" came to the tomb with spices (24:1). He provides no names or further description, so the reader must consult the previous chapter to see who is meant here. Luke reports in 23:55–56 that the women from Galilee followed Joseph to the burial site, then returned to their homes and prepared spices, and rested on the Sabbath. When Luke says in 24:1 that "they" came to the tomb bringing spices, he means these women. They found the stone rolled away, but they did not find the body inside. "Two men in dazzling clothes" appeared, and the women were terrified. The men asked, "Why do you look for the living among the dead? He is not here, but has risen. Remember how he told you . . . that the Son of Man must . . . be crucified, and on the third day rise again" (vv. 4–7). The women did indeed remember Jesus' words. The dazzling men did not specifically tell the women to go and tell the disciples, as in Mark and Matthew, but the women did it anyway. They told the good news to the eleven disciples and "all the rest." Luke finally names the women involved: Mary Magdalene, Joanna, Mary the mother of James, and "the other women with them."

Luke adds a plot twist to his story. The women told the good news to the disciples, but the disciples did not believe them! Their story seemed ridiculous, "an idle tale," or even a sign of mental illness. Peter at least gave the women enough credit to go see for himself; he ran to the tomb and saw the linen cloths, but no body. "He went home, amazed at what had happened" (24:12). Later Luke reports that Jesus appeared to the disciples and they were startled and terrified. They apparently needed to see Jesus directly before they could believe the women were telling the truth (vv. 36–43).

John 20. Finally, in the Fourth Gospel, Mary Magdalene came to the tomb alone. She saw that the stone had been removed, so she went to tell Simon Peter and "the other disciple" that someone had stolen Jesus' body. The two men ran back and saw the linen wrappings, neatly folded, but no body. Body thieves would not have left the grave clothes behind. The two disciples believed, but they did not fully understand what had happened. Meanwhile, Mary met the risen Jesus, who commissioned her to go to the disciples and report that she had seen Jesus alive. (See the next section, on Mary Magdalene, for further discussion of this story.)

In two of the four Gospels, Jesus reveals himself to women, even though they would not have been considered reliable witnesses in that time. In the other two Gospels, the angels tell the women that Jesus was raised. In every Gospel, the women are agents of healing and reconciliation. In Mark and Matthew, they are told to tell the disciples and Peter to go to Galilee, where they would see Jesus. The disciples had fled and Peter had denied knowing Jesus, but those failures no longer mattered. Jesus had been raised. Life had conquered death, fear, shame, embarrassment, and failure. Jesus used the voice and presence of the women to invite the men back into the circle of disciples. They had a chance for a new start. They would find forgiveness and reconciliation, and life would begin again for them.

Diving Deeper

"Many women were also there." The women showed up. They could do little more than watch and wait, so that is what they did.

When someone we love is in a crisis, merely showing up seems insufficient. We do not know what to do, but we assume there must be some tangible action that would be helpful. There are certainly many practical acts of kindness that are important and meaningful. Bringing food, helping with child care, working in the yard. But sometimes, just being present is the greatest gift. Showing up at the hospital to support the family of a patient in intensive care. Taking time to attend the visitation or the funeral. Sitting in silence with the person who is hurting. Choosing to sit in the church pew next to the recently divorced person.

Similarly, when someone we love is eager, happy, and excited, we can show up at their athletic contest, band concert, theater production, or school program. Being present shows support and encouragement and helps to build trusting relationships.

Together. In Matthew, Mark, and Luke, women came to the tomb in a group. In John, Mary Magdalene came alone, but when she saw the stone rolled away, she went to find Peter and another disciple. There was safety in numbers, but they also must have found comfort and support in one another. Their grief was a tiny bit easier to bear in the presence of others who had experienced the same loss.

Remember. The angel in Luke reminded the women to remember what Jesus had taught them. They had what they needed to make sense of these strange events. Jesus had said he would be crucified, and on the third day, he would rise. They did not fully understand it at the time, but now it made more sense.

What do we need to remember? We have been baptized. We have been welcomed into God's family. We are God's beloved. We matter. We are forgiven. We are called. We are gifted. We are worthy. And God extends the same grace to all God's beloved children. Jesus is alive, and his new life gives us new life.

Questions for Reflection and Discussion

What do you think about comparing the resurrection accounts? Is that a threat to faith? Why spend time on this? What might we learn from comparing and contrasting?

Why do the women seem to have a relatively small role in the life of Jesus, but a significant presence at the cross and resurrection? Could they have been more active and present in the life of Jesus than the Gospels record? Why do you think the risen Jesus appeared to women?

How have you experienced the power of faithful presence? How have people shown up for you? How have you shown up for others?

How have you experienced resurrection and new life? Forgiveness and reconciliation?

MARY MAGDALENE
(John 20:1–18)

What do you know about Mary Magdalene?* Is she a prostitute? A disciple? The wife of Jesus? An apostle? A woman possessed by demons? Like many of the women discussed in this book, Mary Magdalene

---

* Mary Magdalene is also mentioned in Matt. 27:56, 61; 28:1–10; Mark 15:40, 47; 16:1–11; Luke 8:1–3; 24:1–12; John 19:25.

appears in only a few verses of Scripture. Unlike others who have no names, or speak briefly if at all, Mary has been remembered. She is the subject of sermons and Bible studies. Even though the biblical evidence about her is minimal, there are many representations circulating in art, theater, novels, movies, and legends. Here are some you might remember.

The best-selling novel *The Da Vinci Code* included a plotline about Mary Magdalene's marriage to Jesus and the child she bore with him. In 1988, the film version of Nikos Kazantzakis's novel *The Last Temptation of Christ* caused a stir because its Jesus imagined what it would have been like to live a normal life and marry Mary Magdalene (who was described as a reformed prostitute). In 1973, the rock opera *Jesus Christ Superstar* portrayed Mary Magdalene as a reformed prostitute who sings "I don't know how to love him" about her romantic attraction to Jesus.[4]

More recently, the television series *Downton Abbey* included an episode about a maid and former prostitute who scandalizes the men of the Crawley family when she serves the women at a luncheon (see chap. 4). One of the male servants says afterward that he could not have eaten a bite in the presence of a prostitute. The housekeeper, Mrs. Hughes, replies that Jesus ate with Mary Magdalene. The servant is not sure about that, but he claims that Jesus did allow her to wash his feet.

If you search online for images of Mary Magdalene, you will find hundreds of paintings. Some portray a beautiful and voluptuous young woman wearing a skimpy red dress and a come-hither look. Others show a sad and miserable penitent, or a pious woman at prayer.

Perhaps you have heard a sermon on Easter Sunday that described Mary as a needy, neurotic woman filled with inappropriate love for Jesus.

Mary Magdalene may be the best-known woman in the New Testament after Mary the mother of Jesus, and yet much of what we think we know about her is completely unsupported by Scripture. She was not a prostitute. She did not wash Jesus' feet. She did not marry Jesus or have his child. She was not a pathetic, sinful woman or a beautiful temptress.

Mary Magdalene is mentioned thirteen times in the New Testament, twelve in connection with the crucifixion or resurrection of Jesus. The other mention occurs during the ministry of Jesus. In Luke 8:2–3, she is named as a benefactor of Jesus and the disciples. She is not identified as any man's wife, daughter, or mother. Rather, she is distinguished from the many other women named Mary by her hometown, Magdala, a fishing village in Galilee. Mary, along with Joanna, Susanna, and many others, ministered to Jesus and the disciples out of their means.

How did these women get the money to provide for Jesus and the disciples? Some interpreters speculate that they must have been prostitutes, because that was the only way women could make money. It is also possible they worked at other jobs, or that they were the widows or daughters of wealthy men.

Some of the women had been cured of evil spirits and infirmities, so they may have joined the disciples as a way to express their gratitude. Mary Magdalene is identified as one of these, having had seven demons cast out of her. Some interpreters paint a horrific picture of Mary as possessed by strong satanic forces, or they claim that the seven demons were actually the seven deadly sins, including greed, sloth, and especially lust. It is more likely that she had a mental illness, such as bipolar disorder or depression, or a physical illness, such as epilepsy.

Regardless of how she came to be there, we know that Mary Magdalene was often present with Jesus and the disciples. She probably functioned as a disciple herself, though she was not considered one of the core group of twelve men who followed and learned from Jesus. As Jesus and the disciples traveled around Galilee, Mary, along with the other women, may have provided a home base where they slept at night. Or the women may have traveled with the men and provided food, water, and other necessities. These two verses (Luke 8:2–3) about the women provide precious little detail, but illustrate the women's devotion to Jesus.

The other twelve references to Mary Magdalene all say that she and other women were present with Jesus at the cross and the burial, and they were the first to appear at the tomb to witness the resurrection. All four Gospels name Mary Magdalene as present at the end of Jesus' life. (See the first part of this chapter for discussion of the references in the Gospels.)

Each of the four Gospels tells the story of Easter morning a bit differently, and with a different combination of women, but Mary Magdalene is mentioned each time. The Gospel of John presents the most detailed story. Jesus had been crucified on a Friday, and his body was put in the tomb at the end of the day, before the Sabbath began at sunset on Friday. Early on the first day of the week (Sunday), Mary went to the tomb alone, to grieve and care for the body of Jesus. The Gospels do not record the details of their relationship, but it is clear from her presence at the cross, burial, and tomb that she cared deeply for Jesus. She took a risk to be present at these places, because it was dangerous to publicly mourn a "criminal."

When Mary arrived, she saw that the stone in front of the tomb had been rolled away, and she concluded that someone had taken the body of Jesus.[5] Without looking inside, she ran to tell Peter and the beloved disciple that the body had been taken. The two men ran back to the tomb, and when they looked in, they saw that the cloths used to wrap his body were folded neatly in a pile. Thieves would not have carefully removed and folded the wrappings! But the men were still puzzled. Something strange had happened, and neither the men nor Mary had any categories to explain the absence of a body, other than theft.

The men went home, unsure of what to do next. Mary stayed. She peered into the tomb and saw two angels sitting where the body of Jesus had been. She was "ugly crying," loud sobs of lament and grief. The angels asked why, and she said that someone had taken away her Lord, and she did not know where they had laid him. She then turned and saw Jesus standing there, but she did not recognize him. Why not? Consider the circumstances. Jesus had died a brutal death, and no one expected to see him again. It may have still been dark, or her tears may have clouded her sight, or his resurrected appearance may have been quite different from the way he looked before. She could only imagine that he was the gardener, and when he also asked why she was weeping, she responded to his compassion with her desperate questions. Did you take him away? Where did you put his body? I want to take care of him.

Then the "gardener" called her by name. "Mary." When she heard her name, she also knew Jesus. What happened to her in that moment of recognition? Everything changed. The dead man was alive. That broken body on the cross was now standing whole in front of her. What a jolt to her body and soul. In the time it took to say her name, she moved from devastating loss and despair to a joy nearly too much to take in. It was, somehow, Jesus.

When Mary recognized Jesus, she called him "Rabbouni," which means teacher. She must have made a move to embrace him, because Jesus said, "Do not hold on to me, because I have not yet ascended to the Father" (John 20:17).

Some preachers and commentators have concluded from this brief exchange that Mary acted inappropriately. They claim that she sought a romantic relationship and wanted to embrace him in an intimate, even sexual, way. They assume that Jesus was scolding her for being emotionally needy, desiring him sexually, and seeking a relationship with him.

The text does not say any of this. Embracing a friend who is alive when you thought he was dead is a completely normal response and says nothing about inappropriate intimacy. In John 20:26–27, Jesus invites Thomas to touch him, and in Matthew 28:9, the women joyfully fall at Jesus' feet. Jesus is not discouraging Mary's embrace so much as he is suggesting she not hang on to him. He had work to do, and could not be confined, or held in place. He is signaling that life for him was different now, and life for Mary would be different too. She could not hold on to Jesus, because she had her own work to do. She needed to go and do the work of an apostle, telling the disciples that she had seen the risen Jesus! They both needed to move on.

Mary Magdalene did as Jesus asked and went to tell the men that she had seen the Lord, and that is the last time she is mentioned in the New Testament. She does not appear in the Acts of the Apostles. She is not named in the apostle Paul's letters as a leader of the early church. She is not mentioned in a list of people who saw the risen Jesus which Paul included in his Letter to the Corinthians (1 Cor. 15:5–8). We do not know why she is absent, especially since several centuries later, the theologian Augustine referred to her as the Apostle to the Apostles. An apostle was someone who had seen the risen Jesus and was chosen to proclaim the good news of the resurrection. Mary was the apostle who first told this good news to the other apostles! She played a significant role, and it is strange that nothing more is said of her.

These few texts tell us that Mary followed Jesus. She cared about him enough to risk her own safety by being present at the cross and the tomb. She felt a powerful sense of loss and grief at his death, she felt great joy when he was raised, and Jesus sent her to bring the good news to the male disciples.

If this is all the information that the text provides, how did Mary pick up so much negative baggage? How did she become known as a fallen women? To put it bluntly, how did Mary Magdalene become a whore?[6]

The confusion started early. The Gospels mention several women named Mary in addition to the mother of Jesus and Mary Magdalene. There is Mary of Bethany, who is the sister of Martha and Lazarus, and several other Marys who are identified by their sons. A serious mix-up occurred in a sermon preached by Pope Gregory the Great around 600 CE. He claimed that the unnamed "sinner" in Luke 7 who washed Jesus' feet with her tears was actually Mary Magdalene, who is mentioned immediately after that story as a benefactor of Jesus (Luke 8:2–3). The woman in Luke 7 was labeled a prostitute or sexual sinner, and thus Mary Magdalene was also labeled a prostitute. The pope claimed that her seven demons were disgusting sexual sins she needed to repent of.

Based on this misinformation, in the centuries since then Mary Magdalene has been portrayed as a seductive, dangerous, glamorous woman. Or she is portrayed as a gaunt, unattractive, penitent sinner who chose a life of humiliation and self-denial to punish herself for her many sins. The Catholic Church tried to set the record straight in 1969 and say that she was not a prostitute, but the label has persisted.[7]

Another source of limited information about Mary Magdalene comes from some of the stories about Jesus and the disciples that did not make it into the Christian Bible, such as the Gospel of Philip, the Gospel of Mary, and the Gospel of Thomas. A common theme in these noncanonical books is that the disciples suspect that Mary has a privileged relationship with Jesus, perhaps even a romantic one, and they resent it. They wonder why Jesus loves her more than them.[8]

These stories are interesting and important because they illustrate possible fault lines in the early church. It is possible that Mary Magdalene became a popular and respected figure in the early church, and some disciples may indeed have resented her. Someone may have wanted to reduce her influence and put her in her place. One effective way to minimize a woman's role is to depict her as a sexual sinner.

Long after the age of the early church, Christians continued to tell stories about Mary Magdalene. Around the thirteenth century, a collection of legends about saints included one about Mary. In it, she, along with Martha, Lazarus, and other early Christians, was sent off on a boat without oars or rudders. Miraculously, they survived, and Mary arrived in Marseilles, France, where she preached the gospel and performed miracles. The legend also claims that she spent the last thirty years of her life in seclusion and penitence, because she saw herself as a sinful woman who needed to demonstrate sorrow for her earlier sins.[9]

There is a lot of uncertainty and ambiguity about Mary Magdalene. Typically, scholars and creative artists have dealt with her in one of three ways. The first is to ignore her. She may have disappeared into obscurity after proclaiming the resurrection on the first Easter, but it seems odd that such a strong and passionate woman would have done nothing more for the cause of the gospel. It is also possible that she was active as an apostle, like Peter and Paul, but her work was not recorded. Perhaps she was a bit of an embarrassment to the early church, which was ambivalent about women in leadership roles. (See the chapters on Acts and Paul's letters.) It was difficult then, as it often is now, to see a woman as independent, intelligent, and strong, rather than as a sexual object who is weak and stupid. It was difficult to see a woman functioning as a coworker or a friend to a man without romanticizing the relationship.

When Mary has not been ignored, she has often been made to look bad. *Jesus Christ Superstar* and *The Last Temptation of Christ* tell a story about a "slutty" Mary Magdalene. She may be a *former* prostitute, but that role still defines her. Some Easter sermons portray her as a neurotic woman who does not understand that she can't marry Jesus.

Even more troubling are the attempts to depict Mary Magdalene as a penitent sinner. She was a very bad woman who committed terrible sexual sins. Then Jesus saved her from her sin. But her sins were so bad that she spent the rest of her life trying to atone for her bad behavior. Some artists in particular portray her as a once beautiful but now ugly woman. She does not bathe. Her hair is a tangled mess. She wears ugly clothes. She starves herself. She is consumed by her shame. A woman so focused on her evil past is not going to be proclaiming the good news of the gospel!

The third way to deal with Mary is the attempt to make her into a wife and mother, as in *The Da Vinci Code*. This may seem liberating, in a way. Mary Magdalene was just a normal woman who married Jesus and had a baby. But this emphasizes Mary's traditional feminine roles as wife and mother. She would have been so busy caring for Jesus and the children that she would not have had time to proclaim the gospel!

Why has it been so difficult to see Mary Magdalene as a strong woman who was a loving friend of Jesus and proclaimed the gospel after his death, like the other apostles? A strong, healthy, intelligent woman who has experienced grace and forgiveness and wants to share that with others? A woman with leadership skills? A woman who is a gifted preacher? The church has not been comfortable with these depictions of Mary. Better a Mary Magdalene who fits the traditional categories of sinful or ashamed or a married mother than a Mary Magdalene who is a preacher, teacher, apostle. The church has trouble with women who are fully human, with some flaws, perhaps, but even more gifts.

Mary Magdalene seems to be just that sort of woman. She had

struggles, but she was healed and set free from them. She used her energy and resources to care for Jesus and the disciples. She was capable of deep friendship. She was the first to see the risen Jesus, who entrusted her with a significant task, to bring the good news to the disciples who had fled from the cross.

Diving Deeper

Apostle to the Apostles. Mary was a strong woman! Jesus must have trusted and respected her. He appeared to her first. He sent her out to proclaim the good news to the demoralized apostles. The Gospels identify her as the first to the tomb. She must have been a strong and respected figure in the early church. Why is she not affirmed for this role?

"Why are you weeping?" She illustrates the power and reality of human grief. Her grief was real. Our grief is real. Death is real. Even the profoundly good news of the resurrection of Jesus does not ease the pain of human loss. In a moving sermon on this text, Nadia Bolz-Weber said that Mary grieved because "to Jesus she wasn't that crazy lady like she was to everyone else. To him she was just Mary, and when Jesus said her name it felt like a complete sentence."[10]

"I despise myself, and repent in dust and ashes" (Job 42:6). If Mary spent most of her life repenting in dust and ashes about how sinful she had been, she would not have had much time or energy to proclaim the gospel! This is such a powerful and problematic view of repentance. The point of the Christian faith is that God forgives, heals, sets people free. God does not demand constant chest-beating. Forgiveness is a new start and does not require permanent wallowing in grief. Even if she had a sinful past (and who doesn't?), why would Christians think it was admirable to wallow in grief over one's bad choices rather than move on? Compare her story to the apostle Peter, who denied Jesus three times and then abandoned Jesus. Nobody portrays Peter as hiding in a cave and moping over his errors. Peter moved on to become a powerful preacher and leader in the early church.

Magdalene equals sinner. The word "Magdalene" has long been linked with sinful women. In Ireland after World War II, a network of laundries was established by the Catholic Church. Girls and women were sent there for various types of disobedience. They might have had a child before marriage or defied their parents, or even looked like they might become promiscuous. The laundries were named after Mary Magdalene, because she was also thought to be a fallen woman! Women and girls could be sent to these places for years and forced to work, often producing quite a profit for the order of nuns that administered the laundries.[11]

Similarly, well-meaning women developed Magdalene Societies in the nineteenth century with the goal of getting women out of prostitution and on to a better life. These organizations helped to continue the misunderstanding of Mary Magdalene.

Was there a Mrs. Jesus? People are intrigued by the connection Mary Magdalene might have had with Jesus. Was Jesus married? Most Jewish men were, so it was unusual if he was single. If not, did he have friendships with women? Romantic relationships? Kazantzakis posed the question about what might have happened if Jesus had chosen a normal life, and people are curious about it. If Jesus is fully human, as Christianity claims, how did he relate to women? He is so respectful and loving to women that surely some of them found him attractive.

Questions for Reflection and Discussion

Why do you think there has been such a fascination with Mary as prostitute, penitent, and wife and mother? What kind of person do you think she was? How might she be a role model now?

What does it mean to be a disciple? An apostle? To follow Jesus?

Could Jesus have been married? Would that change the way you see him?

7

The Book of Acts

A member or visitor in an African American church might observe a number of women sitting together in the front pews, dressed in white dresses and hats. They are known as Mothers of the Church. They are usually over sixty, and they have demonstrated their faith, commitment, authority, and knowledge of the Bible. They are wise and compassionate. They have given time, money, and energy to keep the church going. They may provide a lot of the supportive talk that happens during many sermons in the Black Church. "Preach!" "Well." "That's right." And of course, "Amen." These women are known as spiritual giants in the congregation, and they are respected and sometimes feared.

Many congregations have their strong powerful women, sometimes affectionately referred to as church ladies.[1] They can be any age, and they do everything from child care and cooking to teaching and preaching. They provide much of the unpaid labor that keeps the church running.

The book of Acts also had its church ladies who played significant leadership and ministry roles. Unfortunately, we know very little about them. We only catch a few glimpses of women, but when we do, we see that they are generous, hospitable, wise, and courageous.

The book of Acts follows the four Gospels in the New Testament. It tells a story about the development of the early church in the years following the death, resurrection, and ascension of Jesus. Acts was probably written two or three decades after the events occurred, by the same person who wrote the Gospel of Luke. The title, Acts of the Apostles, suggests a comprehensive history that will discuss all the apostles, but the book actually focuses only on the work of Peter and Paul. Other apostles are mentioned briefly, if at all. Mary Magdalene is not mentioned at all, even though she was sometimes labeled the Apostle to the Apostles and is thought to have brought the gospel to France. Acts should not be read as a comprehensive report of everything that happened in the early church. Much was left out of this account.

This is particularly true of the activities of women. In the Gospel of Luke, the author describes several women who were disciples, recipients of healing, or respected friends of Jesus. Women followed Jesus during his ministry, crucifixion, resurrection, and ascension. Jesus healed women, taught them, and talked with them as equal and intelligent human beings. They heard his message of liberation and actively participated in his work. They were devastated by his death, stunned and joyful about his resurrection, and mystified by his ascension.

We might expect that the early church would follow the example of Jesus and recognize women as equal participants in sharing the good news, but Acts does not identify any woman as an apostle, preacher, deacon, or participant in theological debate. Women are not the main characters of the story. It appears that the church is being built without them.[2]

New Testament scholars who study the role of women in the early church acknowledge the relatively minimal role of women, but they believe there is much more to the story. Elisabeth Schüssler Fiorenza claims that the occasional presence of women in the book of Acts represents the tip of an iceberg. She argues that women were active in the early church, as leaders of house churches, as financial supporters, and as teachers, mentors, and gracious hosts. While only a few women are mentioned by name in Acts, many other unnamed and unrecognized women played significant roles.[3] This might be called the "glass-half-full" approach to biblical interpretation. When the Bible says that men were present, the Greek word for "men" probably includes women as well. Similarly, when a speaker addresses the "brothers" in the audience, women were probably also in the crowd (see chap. 8 on women in the letters of Paul).

Glimpses of Women in Acts

This chapter will explore the ways that women appear in the book of Acts, first the general references and then the specifically named women.

In the beginning of Acts, the followers of Jesus had gathered in a room in Jerusalem to grieve, pray, wait, and console one another. They must have been reeling from the events of the last several weeks, but they chose to be together in one place (Acts 1:12–14). Two Greek words provide a sense of the intense community they experienced. *Homothumadon* means "having the same passion." *Proskartereō* means "to persist, or persevere, or to continue doing something with an intense effort." The first phrase of verse 14 might be translated, "all persisting together."[4] They were bound by their love of Jesus and their curiosity about the future, and by the desire to stick together and see what would happen next. The women present were not merely the wives or daughters of the disciples, but were followers in their own right. They along with the men were persisting together in a mix of love, curiosity, and fear.

What happened next was astounding! The disciples and other friends of Jesus heard a sound like rushing wind, and small flames appeared on their heads, and they all began to speak in other languages. They did not know what to make of this, but they all left their safe space and mingled with the people from many nations who were gathered in Jerusalem to celebrate the festival of Pentecost. The disciples were able to speak to all these visitors in their own languages. Skeptical observers assumed that the disciples were drunk.

The disciple Peter tried to interpret these strange, chaotic events for the crowd. He quoted a lengthy passage from the Old Testament prophet Joel (2:28–32) which predicted that a day was coming when God's Spirit and power would fall on men and women, old and young, slave and free. That day was today! Jesus had ascended into heaven and was no longer with them, but God had sent a new form of divine presence, the Holy Spirit. Like the wind, God's Spirit could not be seen or touched, but its effects could be felt. The Spirit gave all the followers of Jesus the ability to speak the good news of the gospel, regardless of age, sex, or status. This was new. The Jewish priesthood had been limited to a particular group of men who were entrusted with the holy words and actions of faith, but now the Holy Spirit would speak to and through all of God's people. Women had received the Holy Spirit, and they could be equal participants in this new divine activity (Acts 2:14–36).

Guided and motivated by this powerful Spirit, Peter and the other disciples, now called apostles, or sent ones, traveled around telling the good news about Jesus. Both Jewish and Gentile women responded in faith and became Christ-followers (Acts 17:4, 12, 34). Others did not.

In Acts 13:50 some women so vigorously opposed Paul that they forced him to leave town.

When Saul persecuted the early Christians before his conversion (when his name was changed to Paul), he targeted both men and women, which means that Christian women must have been active and public enough to present a threat (Acts 8:1–3). If women were completely inconsequential, if they never spoke up for the faith or performed public acts that identified them as Christian, why would Saul waste his time persecuting them?

Women were drawn to the passion and connections of the early church, and in turn, the Christian community felt a responsibility to provide for widows and others who had no one else to care for them. Tension arose because Gentile or Greek-speaking widows were not being cared for as generously as the Jewish or Hebrew-speaking women. To remedy this, several men were appointed to serve as deacons and manage the practical care of the needy (Acts 6).

The Identified Women in Acts

When I began the research for this chapter, I assumed that many women are named in the book of Acts. I was disappointed to find only a few. Those who do appear are not developed as characters and rarely speak. Still, some women are named, and they are often linked to a specific role in the early church. Each will be described briefly here. As you read the brief biblical references, you might ask these questions: What is significant about these women? What contribution did they make? How might they hint at the presence of others like them, who are not named?

Mary the mother of Jesus (Acts 1:14). Despite her singular role in the life of Jesus and her prominent place in the Roman Catholic Church, the Bible says relatively little about Mary. She is present at the birth of Jesus, obviously, but only a few other times (Mark 3:31; John 2:1–11). The Gospel of Mark hints at some tension in the relationship between Jesus and his family members, who wonder if he is mentally ill. Readers are left wondering what happened to her, but the author of Acts makes it clear that Mary was a follower of Jesus. She was waiting with the rest on the day of Pentecost to see what happened next. Unfortunately, she is never mentioned again.

Sapphira (Acts 5). The early Christian community demonstrated a remarkable level of connection and caring (2:42–47; 4:32–37). People shared their food and goods, and some sold their property and gave the money to the community. As in most communities that seem too good to be true, there were some cracks in this idyllic portrait. Ananias and Sapphira were a married couple who decided to sell some property, but rather than give all the proceeds to the community, they held some back for themselves. That was legitimate, because giving was voluntary, but they pretended they had given the entire amount. Peter accused Ananias of lying not only to the community but also to the Holy Spirit, and immediately Ananias dropped dead. A few hours later, Sapphira came into the room, unaware of her husband's death. She also lied and dropped dead.

This story is difficult because it does not fit with our view of a patient, gracious, forgiving God. Punishment was swift and decisive, and Ananias and Sapphira had no chance to explain or apologize. Why was this sin treated so harshly?

It was dangerous to be a Christian in the first century. Non-Christians perceived Christian faith and practice as foolish, disloyal, and unpatriotic. The Christian community had to be a place of absolute integrity and complete trust. Christians needed to rely on each other to preserve their safety. Ananias and Sapphira were free to donate whatever they chose, but they lied to make themselves look more generous. Their lying and self-promotion threatened the essential values of integrity and honesty. Lying broke trust and faith and insulted the Holy Spirit and the other Christians. Their sin was not so much that they broke a rule, but that they failed to honor and trust in God and the community.

Tabitha (Aramaic name) or *Dorcas* (Greek name; Acts 9:36–43). Little is known about her background except that she had the means to care for the widows in the city of Joppa. She made clothes that were not simply functional, but so beautiful that the recipients were eager to show them off. She was so deeply loved that when she died, her friends sent a messenger to the apostle Peter and asked him to come. When he arrived, he raised her from the dead.

The story illustrates Peter's power to heal, but it also presents a powerful picture of a woman in the early Christian community. Tabitha was respected because she was generous in her care for the weak and vulnerable. She made beautiful clothes because needy people were worthy of quality and beauty. The recipients of care did not need to humbly accept charitable cast-offs that were cheap and ugly.

Tabitha is an example of the way that Christians in the early church valued and cared for each other. She used her resources to help those who had less. Those with resources believed that God had provided them for the specific purpose of sharing, rather than hoarding them. The wealthier people were not to condescend to the poor or share their gifts in a lady- or lord-of-the-manor way. Poor people were not seen as a burden or as wards of the state but as worthy recipients of the resources God had given to some members of the community for the benefit of all. The poor were not to be pitied or resented or given only the minimum resources for survival. The poor provided an opportunity for the wealthier to share. All were valuable members of the community, with a strong sense of connection, identity, and belonging.

Tabitha/Dorcas has long been seen as someone to emulate and honor. My grandmother in Iowa belonged to her church's Dorcas Circle, a group of women who cooked and served and cared for others. Like Tabitha, many women contribute to the work of the church by sewing baptismal banners, knitting prayer shawls, or washing and ironing the paraments. They use their talents to perform tangible acts of compassion, which are much appreciated. Cold hands are warmed by knitted mittens. Cancer patients receiving chemo treatments are comforted by the love and care that created the prayer shawl. Ministers who accidentally spill the wine on the white cloth covering the Communion table appreciate the person who takes the time to clean it. These Tabitha tasks lend warmth and humanity and connection to church life. They should be celebrated. Tabitha is a role model for those who are coordinated, crafty, and creative.

Mary the mother of John Mark (Acts 12:12–17). In this story, the apostle Peter was miraculously released from prison by an angel. When Peter was freed, he immediately sought out the Christian community that met in Mary's home. They had been praying for his well-being. The house had an outer gate, which suggests that it was relatively large, and the text specifies that it was her house, not her son's. People gathered there when they needed the support of the community in a stressful time, and Peter saw it as a safe place to go.

Mary may have been a relatively wealthy woman if she owned a space large enough to fit a couple dozen people. She shared her space and perhaps prepared a meal for the Christians who gathered regularly for worship. She may also have provided leadership for the community worship, by preaching or leading a discussion or presiding at the Lord's Supper. Or she may have taken care of all the organizational details required to keep a group together and functioning, especially in a dangerous environment that required some secrecy. Whatever the details of her role, she provided safe and sacred space in her home for the worshipers to meet. She built community. She helped people encounter God and connect with each other.

A twenty-first-century church lady might also organize church life. One congregation has a program of prayer partners, in which people covenant for six weeks to get to know and pray for each other. The organizer is a church matriarch who knows everyone. She pairs up unlikely people, often of different generations, who might otherwise never get to know each other. She possesses deep wisdom and spiritual presence and seems to know just who might need whom. She may not have a church in her physical house, but she certainly knows how to build community and bring people together.[5]

Rhoda (Acts 12:12–17). She was the maid or servant of Mary (above). Her story provides a touch of comic relief in the midst of sadness and fear over Peter's imprisonment. When Peter came to the gate of Mary's home, Rhoda was so shocked to see him alive and free that she rushed away without letting him in! She went to the worshipers and reported that Peter was at the door, but nobody believed her. They assumed she was out of her mind. Maybe she had seen Peter's angel. Peter kept knocking, and eventually some of the people went to the gate to check, and it was Peter! Finally, they let him in.

Lydia (Acts 16:11–15, 40). She was an early convert who sold purple cloth. The apostle Paul came to Macedonia, his first location in Europe, and met a group of women gathered next to a river outside the city of Philippi. This might have been the location of a Jewish synagogue, as Paul often began work in a new city at the synagogue. Or it may have been a casual group of believers without official status, perhaps because they lacked enough men. Paul sat down with them and taught them. This may have presented something of a challenge to him, if he had been raised to believe that women should not be taught the holy Jewish books. At this point in his life, he taught anyone who listened.

Lydia was one of the women present. She was probably a Gentile who worshiped God along with Jews but had not converted to Judaism. God opened her heart and mind and she believed in the gospel of Jesus. She and her household were baptized, which meant she chose to identify herself fully as a follower of Jesus.

Lydia is identified as a dealer in purple cloth. Owning and wearing purple cloth was a sign of wealth, because the process of dyeing cloth purple was expensive and time-consuming. It was dirty and smelly and usually done on the outskirts of town. There was a difference between purple wearers and purple workers. Lydia may or may not have been wealthy, but she had enough money to own a house and keep servants and run a business.

When she confessed her faith and identified as a Christian, she immediately noticed the practical issues that needed solving. Paul needed a place to stay while he was working in Philippi, so she invited him to stay in her house. She was hospitable. She used her resources in service of the Christian community. She also invited Christians to use her home for a worship space. She probably also exercised leadership in worship.

The girl with the spirit (Acts 16:16–24). While Paul was in Philippi he had an awkward encounter with a young slave girl who was possessed with a spirit that gave her mysterious prophetic powers. She had no name or status, but she was a source of profit for her owners. Oddly, the voice inside her proclaimed that Paul and his coworkers were "slaves of the Most High God" and proclaimed the way of salvation! That seems like good publicity, but Paul found her words annoying and ordered the spirit to come out of her. Her owners were infuriated at the loss of a profitable business, and they had Paul put in jail. Nothing is said of the young woman's welfare. Did the owners keep her? Or leave her behind since she was no longer profitable? Did the Christian community care for her? Did Paul? Did anyone feel responsible for her?

Priscilla (Acts 18:1–3, 18, 24–28). The author briefly refers to a Jewish couple, Priscilla (the diminutive form of the name Prisca, which is used in Rom. 16:3; 1 Cor. 16:19; and 2 Tim. 4:19) and her husband, Aquila. Her name is usually listed first, which is unusual. She may have been freeborn while he was born a slave. Or she may have been better known in the Christian community. Paul met them in Corinth. They were tentmakers, as he was, so they worked together. They also traveled with him to Ephesus. Like Mary and Lydia, Priscilla and Aquila led a church in their house.

Along with her skills in tentmaking and church leadership, Priscilla was a teacher. She and Aquila met a young man named Apollos. He was a preacher of the Christian gospel, but his education had been limited, and there were gaps in his understanding of the Christian faith. Priscilla and Aquila gave Apollos some private tutoring to improve his knowledge base. This is particularly significant because the First Letter to Timothy (written several decades later and probably not by

Paul) insists that women should not teach men! In the last two millennia, some Christian men have argued that women should not teach or preach to men. Some go so far as to say that women should not teach male students in college or high school. Some men are not sure whether they should read commentaries written by women. But in this story, a woman effectively teaches a man.

When these interpreters read about Priscilla, they claim that either Aquila was the actual teacher or her "teaching" was private and personal, little more than spiritual advice from a wise older woman who was nice and nonthreatening. As a woman, Priscilla could not have been teaching theology. That seems like twisting the text to avoid the obvious statement. When Paul was writing, women did function as teachers, which meant they had some authority in the Christian community.

The daughters of Philip (Acts 21:8–9). The text says these women prophesy but includes no details about the content of their speech. The vignette does suggest that women engaged in prophecy.

Women and the Book of Acts

If all the stories about women in the book of Acts were combined, they would fill only one short chapter out of twenty-eight. Given the male-dominated social context of the first century, however, it is surprising they are mentioned at all. Most of the time, men led, men spoke, men decided. And yet, these women led, spoke, and taught. They also sewed and cooked and told the story of Jesus. If some women are mentioned, there were probably many more who did similar things but are not named.

The book of Acts highlights the work of two significant figures, Paul and Peter, but the book also emphasizes teamwork. Peter and Paul do not act alone. They have helpers. And much of the time, the good news is communicated when one ordinary person tells another about Jesus. These ordinary people are not identified, but their conversations are essential to the life and well-being of the church, then and now.

In the beginning the Christian communities were small and intimate. They met in homes, and leadership was flexible. As the church grew, it became more structured. The flexibility of following the Spirit shifted to a greater dependence on rules and structures to maintain order. When worship moved out of homes and into more formal church buildings, the leaders were more likely to be men. Women and slaves played less of a role. As the church gained power, influence, and respectability, it lost sight of the earlier practices of equality and the early recognition that God's Spirit spoke through everyone: women and men, slave and free, young and old.

Diving Deeper

All persisting together. Contemporary Christians might underestimate the uncertainty and anxiety of the disciples at the beginning of Acts. They had experienced the devastating loss of Jesus, then the shocking joy of his resurrection, and then his sudden absence after the ascension. That emotional intensity probably left them exhausted, anxious, and uncertain. Jesus had given them a profound experience of grace and inclusion, and they wanted to pass that experience along to others, but they were not sure how. Jesus had told them to make disciples of all nations, but those broad instructions did not necessarily help them know what to do next.

In the midst of this uncertainty, they persisted together. They shared the same passion for Jesus and the gospel. They were committed to Jesus and to each other. They were not sure what would come next, but they knew enough to stay together and draw strength from each other.

Christians face a similar challenge now. We are exhausted and overwhelmed by the high level of conflict, violence, disease, and pain in the world. We do not know what to do next when society is so dysfunctional. It is difficult to keep caring when there is one crisis after another. We are tempted to give up and focus only on our own lives, families, and friends.

When it feels like the world is falling apart, it is even more important to persist together.

It is important to keep asking how the good news of the gospel speaks to contemporary issues. What would Jesus say about caring for and welcoming immigrants? What would Jesus say about caring for the poor? What would Jesus say about providing access to health care?

Christians will not always agree, just as they did not always agree in the early church. They are still called to persist together and to make a difference in the world. Recently in my community, a gifted musician formed the Persisterhood Choir, a group of women who sang at protests and marches. The choir members recognized that they could not fix every social problem, but they could persist. They could stick together in sisterhood. And they could sing.

Rules of community. The story of Ananias and Sapphira shows that some values could not be violated. Preserving trust and integrity was one of them.

What are the core values and unbreakable rules that shape church communities? For some churches it is the preservation of purity. The church cannot be "soft on sin." For others, the core value is that the gospel includes the marginalized. Members of a single congregation might disagree about the core values and unbreakable rules. Denominations are even more likely to have conflicting values, especially over difficult questions about sexuality. In the midst of these conflicted situations, it might be helpful to dig a little deeper into a church's history, theology, and interpretation of Scripture. Are there passions that bind church members together and transcend the conflicts? Or is it impossible to continue persisting together when one group has core values that the others do not share?

Safe space. Lydia, Mary, and Priscilla all helped to create a safe space for worship and study. This was not just psychologically or aesthetically safe space. In a time when people could die for being Christian, a safe worship space was essential.

Hospitality creates safe space for guests. Lydia invited Paul to stay at her house. Peter knew he could go to Mary's house when he was freed from prison.

All things in common. One of the most radical lines in Acts is this: "There was not a needy person among them, for as many as owned lands or houses sold them and brought the proceeds" (4:34). Christians who had extra resources saw their excess as God's way to provide for the poor. This is a compelling vision of Christian community, and yet it has often been dismissed as idealistic, impossible, or socialist.

When the Puritans sailed to Massachusetts in 1630, their leader, John Winthrop, preached a sermon while they were still on the ship. He reminded them that they had made this dangerous journey over the Atlantic Ocean in order to build a new Christian community. Everything they owned now or would own in the future had been given to them by God for the welfare of the community. God might give some people more resources and others less, but that did not mean the wealthy had worked harder or behaved better or were more deserving. Instead, any extra that an individual possessed beyond the necessities of life was to be shared with those in the community who were poor. Winthrop said, "We must be willing to abridge ourselves of our superfluities, for the supply of other's necessities."[6] This is a radically different and difficult way of looking at our resources.

Questions for Reflection and Discussion

What does hospitality look like? How can we create safe spaces in church, home, and classroom? How can the church create safe space for children, teens, singles, differently abled, the elderly, the poor, and people who are LGBTQ+?

Who have been the influential church ladies in your life? And church men? What have they done, and how? What gifts have they brought to the church? The world?

How do churches change? How do they become more welcoming? Are there limits to change? How do you decide and discern?

What are the core values or unbreakable rules in your church? How did you come to hold those?

What do you think about the radical sharing practiced in the early Christian community? Is it legitimate now for some people to have so much while others have so little?

When have you seen people sharing a passion? All persisting together? In a church? Somewhere else? When you see a deep sense of community and connection and shared purpose, what are the shared values and passions that shape the community?

8

The Letters of Paul

On the last Sunday of the month in the congregation where I worship, the smell of pizza begins wafting into the sanctuary during the prayers of the people. When worship ends, the people move to the commons area to have lunch together. Families volunteer to set up and clean up, but everybody carries their dishes to the kitchen. The suggested donation is one dollar per slice, but some pay more and some pay less. Visitors and college students are invited guests. Senior citizens sit with teenagers. Children play tag. A few people remain deep in conversation long after most others have left. As I look around, I see friendships across generations. I see people who for decades have given time and money to the church. I see children and teens being nurtured by adults who are not their parents. I see people who have faced challenges with grace. I see many gifted, talented, loving people.

That is church for me. Doctrine, worship, ethical life choices, service, and personal spirituality all play a role in church life, but at heart, church is about connections and community. At its best, church is a place where people feel like they belong. They participate, they have a role, they are linked to others, and they are welcomed and loved.

When the apostle Paul writes letters to the early Christian churches, sometimes he teaches theology, sometimes he gives advice about thorny ethical questions, and sometimes he attempts to resolve conflicts. He is also trying to build community and connections, so he greets people and introduces them to each other. He praises and thanks people. He encourages them to care for each other. He knows that the Christian communities are built on webs of relationships. In the first century, and now, women are an essential part of these communities.

In the book of Acts we discovered some of the ways that women were involved in the early church, as prophets, leaders, evangelists, and teachers. Acts describes the travels and ministry of the apostle Paul and mentions some of his coworkers, including Lydia and Priscilla (or Prisca). Acts provides the travelogue, but in Paul's letters to the young Christian communities, we read Paul's own words. Paul wrote letters to the Romans, the Corinthians, the Galatians, the Philippians, the Thessalonians, and Philemon.[1] The letters contain theological reflections, pastoral advice, and personal greetings.

In the first century, communication at a distance was difficult and infrequent. There was a mail system in the Roman Empire, but it was limited to government communication, so people who wanted to convey a long-distance message had to find a courier to deliver it in person. A letter was a significant document, crafted with care. Paul could not casually update a Facebook page every day or send mass emails to his followers. He had to handwrite or dictate a letter, then find a trustworthy person who would travel perhaps hundreds of miles to deliver it. Upon arrival, the courier did not simply leave the letter in a church's mail slot and return home. The courier was expected to read the letter to the recipients, making sure that the spoken tone and inflections expressed exactly what Paul wanted to say.

Paul was in Corinth, near Athens, when he wrote the Letter to the Romans around 58 CE. Paul had never been to Rome, but he intended to visit, in part because he wanted to use Rome as a base for his next missionary journey, to Spain. He hoped to receive financial and moral support from the Roman Christians. To build a relationship with them, Paul wrote an extensive account of his understanding of the Christian faith. Romans is his longest letter, and the most theologically dense and substantive. He was trying to make a good impression.

Paul wanted the letter to arrive before he did, so he had to choose a courier. He could not simply send this letter with anyone who happened to be going to Rome. He had to find someone courageous and respected who could manage the physical demands of a trip of six hundred miles over water and land. The person would have to visit a number of house churches. Most importantly, the courier needed to read the letter the way that Paul would if he were there.

Paul chose Phoebe. She must have been a woman of substance who was strong, confident, wise, courageous, and financially secure. She set off on a long journey to deliver Paul's letter to the church in Rome.

The letter is somewhat unusual because after all the dense theology about sin and redemption, Paul includes an entire chapter of greetings at the end. He mentions twenty-nine people, nineteen men and ten women. How does he know this many people in a city he has never visited? He met some people on his travels who now live in Rome. Some may be friends of friends. Some he knows by reputation. He is trying to establish his status and authority and make connections so that he can build relationships and ask for contributions from the people in Rome.

The fact that Paul mentions so many women makes the list of greetings particularly striking. He names Phoebe, Prisca, Mary, Persis, Junia, Tryphaena, Tryphosa, Julia, Rufus's mother, and Nereus's sister. Readers might find that their eyes glaze over when reading lists of names, and it is easy to skim through the list without realizing how many women are included and why they are significant. The list of names suggests that Paul recognized and valued the work women were doing in the early church.

One of the challenges in reading Paul is that, to put it kindly, he is of two minds. He contradicts himself. At times Paul places strict limits on the roles that women can play in the early church. In 1 Corinthians he writes, "Women should be silent in the churches. For they are not permitted to speak, but should be subordinate, as the law also says. If there is anything they desire to know, let them ask their husbands at home" (14:34–35).[2] Earlier in this letter, however, Paul tells women that when they prophesy or speak in church gatherings, they should wear veils (11:4–15). Here he assumes they will speak in public! Why does he command silence only three chapters later? Why would Paul prohibit women's speech, especially when Acts has shown women exercising leadership in churches?

Paul and other early Christian leaders knew Christianity had a radical, destabilizing quality. Jesus challenged the status quo and treated women, slaves, and other despised people as fully human and valuable in God's eyes. Peter preached on the day of Pentecost that the Holy Spirit would fall on men and women, slaves and free, old and young. The Roman Empire might be threatened by such radical equality, and in order to minimize the threat, Paul insisted that women wear veils. Some Christian women may have concluded that their freedom in Christ meant that they no longer needed to wear veils as a sign of their modesty and submission. Paul insisted that they follow the rules of

Roman society and continue to be appropriate and modest rather than flaunting their freedom in Christ.

Paul may have advised silence in response to a particular situation in Corinth. The Christians there were a feisty bunch. Many of them were convinced that the Holy Spirit was speaking through them, so worship could be chaotic as multiple people competed to convey their particular word from the Lord (1 Cor. 12–14). Spouses may have been calling back and forth to each other during worship, and if men and women were sitting separately, as was the practice in Jewish synagogues, there might have been a great deal of noise and confusion. Paul may have advised women to keep quiet in this particular situation, but he did not necessarily intend to establish a permanent rule for all churches in all times.

Paul also may have been reluctant to allow uneducated women to take on significant leadership roles in the churches. Most women in the first century could not read, let alone engage in the kind of rigorous Scripture study that Paul had experienced. Women had been trained to be wives and mothers, not church leaders and religious scholars. Paul also might have been concerned that uneducated women would be more susceptible to religious ideas that he considered heretical.

Paul may have had what he considered valid reasons to encourage women to be quiet in the Corinthian church. But it is clear from other biblical evidence that this was not Paul's last and most definitive word on the subject. Women did speak and lead in Paul's churches. They were respected. They knew enough to teach. They worked hard alongside Paul in ministry. After Pentecost, women were led by the Holy Spirit, just as men were. They spoke, led, and prophesied.

In Romans 16, Paul identifies ten women as his friends or colleagues in ministry. He respects and appreciates their work and their endurance of suffering. Paul does not hesitate to include them in this list of significant people in the church.

First and foremost was **Phoebe**, the bearer of the letter. Paul introduces her to the various congregations who will hear her read the letter and asks that they support her, provide hospitality, and listen carefully. She is not labeled as any man's wife or daughter, but as a church leader in her own right.

Paul uses three words to describe her. Phoebe is a "sister." Christians in the early church called each other brother and sister as a sign of regard and welcome. The church was a family, a place of intimacy and connection. Some Christians had been disowned by their family members for aligning with a faith that was not only embarrassing but dangerous. Christians then formed new families of kinship and support and remained faithful to their new siblings, even in the midst of persecution. A woman like Phoebe, who may not have had a man in her life, could have found safety and security in the church family. She could be respected and valued, which was not always true for single women in that society.

Paul calls Phoebe a *diakonos*, a Greek word that can mean minister, deacon, or servant. When the word is used in reference to a man, it is often translated as minister (Eph. 6:21; Col. 1:7; 4:7; 1 Tim. 4:6). The Living Bible (TLB), a paraphrase from the 1970s, refers to Timothy the *diakonos* as "worthy pastor" (1 Tim. 4:6). But in Romans 16:1, when *diakonos* is used for a woman, it is translated "deacon" (NRSV, NIV), "deaconess," "servant," or even "dear Christian woman" (TLB). How can the same Greek word be translated so differently?

Phoebe is a *diakonos* of a church in Cenchreae, near Corinth. The word suggests that she is a minister or leader. Phoebe seems to be an exceptionally talented woman who can take on a number of different tasks and do them efficiently and gracefully. She may have had a house of a size to accommodate the people who regularly gathered in a house church. Phoebe may have been the worship leader, the preacher, the organizer, or the pastor of this community. She may have set up the room for worship, prepared the elements for Eucharist, and arranged for a shared meal. Whatever the details, having a church in one's house probably meant some significant leadership roles.

Some commentators have been uncomfortable with this kind of role for Phoebe, so they have translated *diakonos* as "servant" or in the feminine form as "deaconess." Starting around the second century, there was an office of deaconess that was held by older widows who vowed not to remarry and devoted themselves to God and the care of the poor. This is probably not the role Phoebe played. It is more likely that she was the leader or minister of the church and was recognized for her wisdom and authority.[3]

Finally, Paul says that Phoebe is *prostatis*. This Greek word appears only once in the New Testament. It literally means "standing before," and according to nonbiblical evidence it can mean a presider, a patron, or a benefactor who possesses financial resources, power, and authority. Phoebe was likely generous with money and advice, and Paul called her a benefactor of many people, including him. That has made some commentators nervous. Did Phoebe have authority over Paul? That would be impossible! So the word has frequently been weakened and translated as a helper or assistant or even a good friend! These words reduce the woman who likely provided significant financial support for Paul to an aide or personal caregiver who prepares his meals and washes his clothes![4]

Phoebe receives only a brief mention in Paul, yet the words he chooses to describe her suggest that she was a powerful and influential woman in the early church.

Paul next mentions **Prisca** and her husband, Aquila, his coworkers. In Acts she is called Priscilla, which is the diminutive or affectionate nickname. The couple had been exiled from Rome, met Paul in Ephesus, and traveled with him to Corinth. They returned to Rome, and Paul sent his greetings to them via the letter. They had worked with Paul as tentmakers, and they also worked with him in ministry. They had risked their lives for Paul, and he and the Gentile churches were grateful to them. Like Phoebe, they had a church in their house.

Prisca was a woman of many talents. She was a tentmaker, and sewing the canvas material was more difficult than doing delicate embroidery. She also had to travel, often under duress when they were forced to leave a town. She moved from Rome to Ephesus to Corinth to Rome, which required a lot of packing, adjustments, flexibility, and the ability to make friends quickly. She had restarted her life several times.

Paul also notes that Prisca was a woman of courage and fortitude, because she and Aquila had "risked their necks" for Paul's sake (Rom. 16:4). He does not provide the details but obviously is grateful to them for their support and encouragement and possibly direct intervention on his behalf.

Prisca and Aquila have a church in their house, but there is no evidence that Aquila is the spiritual leader while she makes the ham-on-buns for lunch. She teaches Apollos (Acts 18:26) along with her husband. She makes tents. She is a coworker. This does not sound like a woman who has been told to keep silence and ask her husband at home if she has questions. She is a church leader.

In Romans 16:7 Paul asks the Roman Christians to "greet Andronicus and **Junia**, my relatives who were in prison with me." "Relative" probably means fellow Jews rather than blood kin, but the three have a powerful bond, in part because they had been in prison together.

Commentators debate the gender of Junia. Paul says that both Andronicus and Junia are "prominent among the apostles," which suggests that they were well-known apostles. Some commentators conclude that Junia cannot possibly be a woman because women cannot be apostles. They insist the name must actually be the male name Junias.[5] Scholars who study first-century Roman life, however, have found 250 references on tombstones and in other records to women named Junia, but no evidence at all of a man named Junias. Andronicus and Junia were mostly likely a married couple who had met Paul at some point in his travels and had been thrown in prison along with him. Paul respects Junia's long history in the faith and the gifts she uses in service of the church.

If Junia is almost irrefutably a woman, some commentators deny that she is an apostle. Skeptics argue that "prominent among the apostles" means she was well-known *by* the apostles, not an apostle herself. Scholars in the first five centuries of the church usually said that she was an apostle who had seen Jesus and then proclaimed the good news about him.[6] Several sixteenth-century writers argued that a woman could not have been an apostle and insisted that she was merely well-known.[7] Other commentators picked up this thread and decided that Junia may have engaged in general mission work but certainly was not an apostle.

This may seem like hairsplitting, but it is a significant argument. If Paul is indeed acknowledging Junia as an apostle, then a woman held the most significant position in the early church. Apostles were those like Peter and the other disciples who had actually seen the risen Christ and were sent out to proclaim the good news. Paul was also an apostle, although he had not seen the risen Jesus directly but heard his voice on the road to Damascus. If Junia was an apostle, then a woman could hold this significant and respected position, and other women, Mary Magdalene perhaps, could be apostles also. These women might have preached the good news of Jesus Christ just as the male apostles did.

These commentators illustrate the danger of approaching the text with certain assumptions. They believed women could not be apostles, therefore either Junia was not a woman or was not an apostle. They expended a great deal of mental energy to make the text fit their preconceived notions of what women did in the early church! It requires less twisting and manipulating to agree with authors closer to the actual events who acknowledge Junia as an apostle and leader.

The remaining seven women named are given an even briefer description or none at all. Still, their appearance is noteworthy. Paul extends greetings to **Mary**, **Tryphaena** and **Tryphosa**, and **Persis**, and notes that they have all "worked hard in the Lord." Paul praises these women for their diligent efforts alongside him in the ministry. Are they preaching, evangelizing, teaching? These are the tasks that Paul is doing while he works hard for the sake of the gospel, so it makes sense to assume that these women Paul affirms as hard workers are not simply cooking meals or darning clothes, challenging and important as those roles can be. These women are doing ministry.[8]

Paul also affirms the **mother of his friend Rufus**, who has been like a mother to him also. He values relationships and knows that emotional support and encouragement are essential for the hard work he is doing. Finally he praises **Julia** and the **sister of Nereus**, without providing further information about them.

In the Letter to the Philippians, Paul refers to **Euodia** and **Syntyche** as his coworkers (the literal meaning of the Greek word is "together-athletes"!) who struggled with him in the work of the gospel. Paul also exhorts them "to be of the same mind," so they are often remembered as an example of church conflict, or as ornery women who cannot get along (4:2–3). Conflict happens in the Christian community, among women and men. But their disagreement should not distract from the more important fact that Paul refers to them as coworkers with him.[9]

It is often assumed that women's participation in the early church involved little more than care of other women and the poor. The evidence in Acts and Romans suggests that women did exercise leadership. The few names and minimal descriptions are likely only the tip of the iceberg. Instead of dismissing these names as irrelevant or trivial or exceptional examples of minor roles, it seems more appropriate to see these names as representative of a large iceberg below the surface, women who were active in the early church as leaders, apostles, ministers, benefactors, and teachers. In the late fourth century, the preacher John Chrysostom said about the women mentioned in Romans, "The women of those days were more spirited than lions, sharing with the Apostles their labors for the gospel's sake."[10]

Diving Deeper

Deacon, minister, servant. The word *diakonos* can be translated as deacon, minister, or servant. Those words now have very different connotations in the life of the church. The minister is the one in charge who preaches and leads worship and manages the life of the church. In some churches (Methodist, Episcopal), deacon is a transitional office leading to the ministry. In others it is a significant office for laypeople (the Baptist Deacon Board). In other denominations (Presbyterian, Reformed), it is an office for laypeople that focuses on practical forms of ministry, such as collecting the offerings and caring for the church building. A servant lacks official status but quietly works hard at tasks that don't receive much recognition and affirmation: washing the coffee cups, vacuuming, caring for infants in the nursery.

It would be helpful in the life of the church to recognize that one word, *diakonos*, describes all those roles. The minister's role is not to be the center of attention but to serve and empower and care for the people. The servant who does seemingly menial tasks is ministering to the life of the church by doing work that enables all the other work to get done. The deacons who offer practical care to those outside the church by working in the homeless shelter or the food pantry or administering the church budget are engaged in both ministry and service. All of these gifts are important to the life of the church

Coworkers. Paul repeatedly refers to other Christians, male and female, as his coworkers, or as people who have worked hard in ministry. Paul knows that ministry is a cooperative effort. He is also quick to praise and affirm people. All of us value being appreciated. One of the best traits of a leader is the ability to affirm people and enable them to work together.

She is called . . . minister, benefactor, teacher, apostle. Women exercised leadership in the early church, and yet the Christian tradition has long been reluctant to ordain women as ministers and place them in positions of denominational or educational leadership. That resistance has slowly changed since 1853 when Antoinette Brown was ordained a minister in the Congregational Church. Most mainline Protestant denominations now ordain women as ministers, although women are more likely to serve as associate pastors, chaplains, and pastors of small churches than they are to be heads of staff in large congregations.

If women can be ministers, is there no longer a need for the Dorcas Circle? The women's group? Sewing groups? The group that prepares the funeral lunches? Are the old roles for women irrelevant now? Do the women who faithfully served the church their whole lives—cooking, teaching, fund-raising, knitting, sewing—still have anything to offer? All these gifts have kept the church running and financially afloat for centuries. The work women have done is essential to the life of the church.

To invite women to roles of preacher, teacher, worship leader, administrator, and counselor does not necessarily denigrate these other roles, and yet it has often been viewed that way. All gifts are important, and they do not need to be gendered. Men do not automatically get to lead and preach and be senior pastors just because they are men. Women do not automatically have to cook and clean and care for the children just because they are women. But even the way I phrase that shows how much more value we put on leading, teaching, preaching, and being in charge, and less value on other kinds of tasks, even though they are no less essential in the life of the church.

"More spirited than lions"! Women have always been a significant presence in the life of religious communities. Who are the spirited women whom you know? What makes them spirited?

Questions for Reflection and Discussion

Have your views about women in leadership changed over time?

How do we discern gifts in a way that isn't based on gender expectations?

How do we nurture women who are leaders? Men who care for children and make the coffee? How can we move to valuing all the work of the church equally? Is it possible?

What is the most meaningful aspect of church for you?

What Would Jesus Do?

God isn't looking for servants. God isn't looking for slaves, workers, contestants to play the game or jump the hoops correctly. God is simply looking for images! God wants images of God to walk around the earth! . . .

God wants *useable instruments* who will carry the mystery, . . . who can bear the darkness and the light, who can hold the paradox of incarnation—flesh and spirit, human and divine, joy and suffering, at the same time, just as Jesus did. Watch what Jesus does, and do the same thing!

—Richard Rohr, *Things Hidden: Scripture as Spirituality*

Group Discussion Guide

MARK PRICE

INTRODUCTION

The author of *From Daughters to Disciples: Women's Stories from the New Testament*, Lynn Japinga, describes the Bible as a mirror: "It is a mirror in which we see first-century people struggling with some of the same issues that we experience today: the power of human sin to hurt others and ourselves, the power of shame and guilt, and the power of grace and love to heal and to make new. In Scripture we see Jesus modeling courageous and healthy ways of living. We see human beings modeling selfish, greedy, and mean-spirited ways of living. We also see human beings who are transformed by the love of Jesus and the power of the Holy Spirit. We see grace. We see love. We see God."

To begin your study of these stories and Japinga's commentary on them, encourage your group to use this metaphor of a mirror in reading the biblical text. Keep these basic questions in mind: *In these women's stories, where do we see grace? Where do we see love? Where do we see God?*

Unlike the stories of women in the Old Testament, the stories of women in the New Testament do not provide much material to work with. The women are often not named and do not speak. The text does not describe how they feel or what they think. Particularly in the Gospels, the women are present in ways that provide Jesus an opportunity to engage them, heal, or say something profound. Because of that, the author suggests approaching these stories imaginatively, even speculatively, looking for points of connection and places where the stories resonate with your own experiences.

This discussion guide uses the following format for the six sessions.

Gathering   5 minutes

Welcome and Prayer. Begin on time by welcoming the group to the study. To open the first session together, be prepared to summarize

123

as briefly as possible what participants can expect from the study and what is expected of them. Then establish a particular ritual of praying together at the start of the study. Keep in mind that the text of this study, the Bible, is a rich source of meaningful prayers, including prayers by some of the women characters (Mary, for example) the group will discuss. A suggestion of a Scripture prayer will appear in this section each week.

Engaging the Text (Bible)   10 minutes

This study guide corresponds to the eight chapters of the book, each one highlighting women grouped, first, by order of appearance in the Gospel writers' narratives of Jesus and, then, canonically from Acts through Paul's letters. The biblical passages covered in each chapter will be listed here. Hear the passage(s) read aloud and then invite group discussion. Consider reading these passages from *The Jewish Annotated New Testament*, second edition, edited by Amy-Jill Levine and Marc Z. Brettler (Oxford: Oxford University Press, 2017). The marginal notes offer needful commentary on understanding the Jewish context out of which the Gospel narratives are told. Some of the marginal notes may be worth lifting up for the group to hear and discuss.

Engaging the Commentary (Book)   20 minutes

The author recalls and comments on the women who appear in the listed passages. Her comments often highlight one of her undergirding assumptions about women and Jesus: that many of the stories depict women as shamed, shunned, submissive, or mistreated within or by their culture. One avenue for group exploration is how women's experiences with Jesus, or with the apostles, or among the earliest followers of Jesus challenge cultural conventions. Suggested questions are provided here to guide the group's responses.

Diving Deeper   15 minutes

As part of her commentary about each woman, the author offers several concluding insights. Make use of those insights in these sections and the reflection questions that follow to prompt the group to share and explore its own insights into each woman's story.

Looking Further   5 minutes

Women's Bible Commentary, 3rd edition, edited by Carol A. Newsom, Sharon H. Ringe, and Jacqueline Lapsley (Louisville, KY: Westminster John Knox Press, 2012), is a volume of biblical interpretation written by women scholars whose comments address passages from every book of the Bible that have particular relevance to women. As a way to wrap up discussion, invite the group to hear and briefly respond to an excerpt from that volume (or, as noted, the first edition, 1992) printed here.

Closing

Turn to the next chapter and preview the focus of the readings for the week ahead.

SESSION 1

The Birth of Jesus

Gathering   **5 minutes**

Greet each other. Begin by praying these words of Mary from Luke 1:46–48:

> My soul magnifies the Lord,
>   and my spirit rejoices in God my Savior,
> for he has looked with favor on the lowliness of his servant.

Engaging the Text (Bible)   **10 minutes**

Choose one or more of the following passages to read aloud.

—Mary, Mother of Jesus (Luke 1:26–56; 2)
—Elizabeth (Luke 1:5–23, 39–45, 57–80)
—Anna (Luke 2:36–38)

Invite discussion of the women in these stories using these questions: *In these women's stories, where do you see grace? Where do you see love? Where do you see God? Where do you see yourself?*

Engaging the Commentary (Book)   **20 minutes**

Ask the group to consider the author's comments on Mary, Elizabeth, and Anna in light of these two questions: (1) What common assumptions or misconceptions about these women and their stories does the author critique? (2) What new ways of understanding these stories do her comments suggest? Discuss as many of the author's comments as time allows.

Diving Deeper   **15 minutes**

Call attention to the "Diving Deeper" sections throughout this chapter and invite discussion of the author's insights about each woman, using

the reflection questions that appear at the conclusion of each section. Work through as many of the questions as time allows.

Looking Further   5 minutes

"Mary is commissioned to be a mother, not a prophet. Her response is to consent freely to motherhood (1:38). With this expression of consent in faith, Luke creates the positive portrait of Mary as model believer. At the same time, Mary's characterization of herself as the 'slave' of the Lord is the text most responsible for the impression of her as a passive character, the antithesis of a liberated woman" (Jane D. Schaberg and Sharon H. Ringe, *Women's Bible Commentary*, 503).

Closing

Turn to the next chapter and preview the next session's readings.

SESSION 2
The Healed

Gathering   **5 minutes**

Greet each other. Begin by praying these words from Acts 4:29–31:

> Now, Lord, . . . grant to your servants to speak your word with all
> boldness, while you stretch out your hand to heal, and signs and
> wonders are performed through the name of your holy servant Jesus.

Engaging the Text (Bible)   **10 minutes**

Choose one or more of the following passages to read aloud.

— The Bold Bleeding Woman (Mark 5:21–43)
— The Bent-Over Woman (Luke 13:10–17)

Invite discussion using some of these questions: *In these women's stories,
where do you see grace? Where do you see love? Where do you see God?
Where do you see yourself?*

Engaging the Commentary (Book)   **20 minutes**

Ask the group to consider the author's comments on the healed women
in light of these two questions: (1) What common assumptions or
misconceptions about these women and their stories does the author
critique? (2) What new ways of understanding these stories do her
comments suggest? Discuss as many of the author's comments as time
allows.

Diving Deeper   **15 minutes**

Call attention to the "Diving Deeper" sections throughout this chapter
and invite discussion of the author's insights about each woman, using
the reflection questions that appear at the conclusion of each section.
Work through as many of the questions as time allows.

Looking Further   **5 minutes**

"The ancient patriarchal world was hierarchical in multiple dimensions: gender, ethnicity, religious status, economic status, political status, and class, which could combine many of these aspects. Mark challenges many of these hierarchies in the status quo of its day, and more recent feminist interpreters have drawn attention to this larger systemic challenge" (Elizabeth Struthers Malbon, *Women's Bible Commentary*, 480).

Closing

Turn to the next chapter and preview the next session's readings.

SESSION 3

The Outcasts

Gathering   **5 minutes**

Greet each other. Begin by praying these words from Jesus' model
prayer in Luke 11:4:

> Forgive us our sins,
> for we ourselves forgive everyone indebted to us.
> And do not bring us into temptation.

Engaging the Text (Bible)   **10 minutes**

Choose one or more of the following passages to read aloud.

— The Syro-Phoenician Woman (Mark 7:24–30; Matt. 15:21–28)
— The Samaritan Woman (John 4:1–42)
— The Woman Caught in Adultery (John 8:1–11)

Invite discussion using some of these questions: *In these women's stories,
where do you see grace? Where do you see love? Where do you see God?
Where do you see yourself?*

Engaging the Commentary (Book)   **20 minutes**

Ask the group to consider the author's comments on the outcasts in
light of these two questions: (1) What common assumptions or misconceptions about these women and their stories does the author critique?
(2) What new ways of understanding these stories do her comments
suggest? Discuss as many of the author's comments as time allows.

Diving Deeper   **15 minutes**

Call attention to the "Diving Deeper" sections throughout this chapter
and invite discussion of the author's insights about each woman, using

the reflection questions that appear at the conclusion of each section. Work through as many of the questions as time allows.

Looking Further   5 minutes

Luke "is often called 'the Gospel of the poor,' just as it is called 'the Gospel of women,' meaning that Luke's concern for the marginalized and oppressed is apparent. It is important to analyze the link between these concerns, since most of the poor in every age are women and the children who are dependent on them" (Jane D. Schaberg and Sharon H. Ringe, *Women's Bible Commentary*, 496).

Closing

Turn to the next chapter and preview the next session's readings.

SESSION 4

The Grateful

Gathering   **5 minutes**

Greet each other. Begin by praying these words from Romans 15:13:

> May the God of hope fill you with all joy and peace in believing, so
> that you may abound in hope by the power of the Holy Spirit.

Engaging the Text (Bible)   **10 minutes**

Choose one or more of the following passages to read aloud.

— The Woman Who Anointed Jesus (Mark 14:3–9; Matt. 26:6–
13)
— The Grateful Woman (Luke 7:37–50)

Invite discussion using some of these questions: *In these women's stories,
where do you see grace? Where do you see love? Where do you see God?
Where do you see yourself?*

Engaging the Commentary (Book)   **20 minutes**

Ask the group to consider the author's comments on the grateful
women in light of these two questions: (1) What common assumptions or misconceptions about these women and their stories does the
author critique? (2) What new ways of understanding these stories do
her comments suggest? Discuss as many of the author's comments as
time allows.

Diving Deeper   **15 minutes**

Call attention to the "Diving Deeper" sections throughout this chapter
and invite discussion of the author's insights about each woman, using
the reflection questions that appear at the conclusion of each section.
Work through as many of the questions as time allows.

Looking Further   5 minutes

"Consistent with the Gospel's [Matthew's] interest in restoring to
full dignity those marginalized or stigmatized by the prevailing social
system, Jesus proclaims [in Matt. 21:28–32] that members of two
despised groups—tax collectors and sinners—epitomize the new faithful. . . . Unlike the 'chief priests and elders' (21:23) ensconced in the
Temple and secure in their status, the tax collectors and prostitutes,
who accepted John the Baptist's message (21:32), will be welcomed
into the realm of heaven" (Amy-Jill Levine, *Women's Bible Commentary*, 1st ed., 347).

Closing

Turn to the next chapter and preview the next session's readings.

SESSION 5

The Sisters

Gathering   **5 minutes**

Greet each other. Begin by praying these words from 2 Thessalonians 3:5:

> May the Lord direct your hearts to the love of God and to the stead-
> fastness of Christ.

Engaging the Text (Bible)   **10 minutes**

Choose one or more of the following passages to read aloud.

— Mary and Martha, Part 1 (Luke 10:38–42)
— Mary and Martha, Part 2 (John 11:1–44; 12:1–8)

Invite discussion using some of these questions: *In these women's stories, where do you see grace? Where do you see love? Where do you see God? Where do you see yourself?*

Engaging the Commentary (Book)   **20 minutes**

Ask the group to consider the author's comments on Mary and Martha in light of these two questions: (1) What common assumptions or misconceptions about these women and their stories does the author critique? (2) What new ways of understanding these stories do her comments suggest? Discuss as many of the author's comments as time allows.

Diving Deeper   **15 minutes**

Call attention to the "Diving Deeper" sections throughout this chapter and invite discussion of the author's insights about each woman, using the reflection questions that appear at the conclusion of each section. Work through as many of the questions as time allows.

Looking Further   5 minutes

"Jesus' conversations with Mary and Martha transform this story from a miracle story about the raising of Lazarus into a story about the fullness of new life that is possible to all who believe in Jesus. For John, the initiative of these women in sending for Jesus, their bold and robust faith, the grief and pain that they bring to Jesus, their willingness to engage Jesus in conversation about life, death, and faith, and their unfaltering love for Jesus are marks of discipleship" (Gail R. O'Day, *Women's Bible Commentary*, 524).

Closing

Turn to the next chapter and preview the next session's readings.

SESSION 6

The Cross and the Empty Tomb

Gathering   **5 minutes**

Greet each other. Begin by praying these words from Psalm 22:1–2, prayed by Christ on the cross:

> My God, my God, why have you forsaken me?
> > Why are you so far from helping me, from the words of my
> > groaning?
> O my God, I cry by day, but you do not answer;
> > and by night, but find no rest.

Engaging the Text (Bible)   **10 minutes**

Choose one or more of the following passages to read aloud. Because these passion narrative sections are lengthy, consider multiple readers.

—The Women and the Cross and Resurrection (Mark 14–16; Luke 22–24)
—Mary Magdalene (John 20:1–18)

Invite discussion using some of these questions: *In these women's stories, where do you see grace? Where do you see love? Where do you see God? Where do you see yourself?*

Engaging the Commentary (Book)   **20 minutes**

Ask the group to consider the author's comments on the women at the cross and the empty tomb in light of these two questions: (1) What common assumptions or misconceptions about these women and their stories does the author critique? (2) What new ways of understanding these stories do her comments suggest? Discuss as many of the author's comments as time allows.

Diving Deeper   15 minutes

Call attention to the "Diving Deeper" sections throughout this chapter and invite discussion of the author's insights about each woman, using the reflection questions that appear at the conclusion of each section. Work through as many of the questions as time allows.

Looking Further   5 minutes

"As women mediate both a man's entry into this world by giving birth and, in many traditions, his exit by participating in funerary rites, women frame the life of Jesus: they are present in his genealogy and the story of his birth, and they are the primary witnesses to his death and resurrection. . . . Matthew records of the Eleven that 'some doubted' (28:17), but of the women Matthew reports only their legitimate fear and their joy" (Amy-Jill Levine, *Women's Bible Commentary*, 477).

Closing

Turn to the next chapter and preview the next session's readings.

SESSION 7
The Book of Acts

Gathering   **5 minutes**

Greet each other. Begin by praying these words of Peter and John in Acts 4:29–30:

> And now, Lord, . . . grant to your servants to speak your word with all boldness, while you stretch out your hand to heal, and signs and wonders are performed through the name of your holy servant Jesus.

Engaging the Text (Bible)   **10 minutes**

Choose one or more of the following passages to read aloud.

    —Tabitha/Dorcas (Acts 9:36–43)
    —Lydia (Acts 16:11–15, 40)
    —The Girl with the Spirit (Acts 16:16–24)

Invite discussion using some of these questions: *In these women's stories, where do you see grace? Where do you see love? Where do you see God? Where do you see yourself?*

Engaging the Commentary (Book)   **20 minutes**

Ask the group to consider the author's comments on women in Acts in light of these two questions: (1) What common assumptions or misconceptions about these women and their stories does the author critique? (2) What new ways of understanding these stories do her comments suggest? Discuss as many of the author's comments as time allows.

Diving Deeper   **15 minutes**

Call attention to the "Diving Deeper" sections throughout this chapter and invite discussion of the author's insights about each woman, using

the reflection questions that appear at the conclusion of each section. Work through as many of the questions as time allows.

Looking Further   5 minutes

"In Philippi Paul found a gathering composed *exclusively* of women. Luke offers no comment on this gathering apart from this mention of it in relation to Paul's itinerary. Even this brief reference, however, opens up a whole new way of envisioning the lives of first-century Christian women. . . . This Sabbath gathering suggests that as early as the first century, women believers sought ways to hear their own voices and stories in worship, freed from the dictates of the male-dominated church" (Gail R. O'Day, *Women's Bible Commentary*, 1st ed., 397).

Closing

Turn to the next chapter and preview the next session's readings.

SESSION 8

The Letters of Paul

Gathering   **5 minutes**

Greet each other. Begin by praying Paul's words from Ephesians 3:16–19:

> I pray . . . that Christ may dwell in your hearts through faith, as you are being rooted and grounded in love. I pray that you may have the power to comprehend, with all the saints, what is the breadth and length and height and depth, and to know the love of Christ that surpasses knowledge, so that you may be filled with all the fullness of God.

Engaging the Text (Bible)   **10 minutes**

Choose one or more of the following passages to read aloud.

—Romans 16
—1 Corinthians 14:26–40; 1 Timothy 2:11–15

Because of the lack of much story detail in the first two passages, relative to the women mentioned, invite speculative discussion about the contributions to the early church made by women acting as deacons, teachers, benefactors, and coworkers with Paul and other early church missionaries. Talk about what barriers they likely faced. Make use of the third passage (Paul's admonition that women remain "silent in the churches," 1 Cor. 14:34), to prompt discussion about how to make sense of Paul's prohibitive words here in light of the other two passages (Rom. 16) where Paul greets and praises his women coworkers.

Engaging the Commentary (Book)   **20 minutes**

Ask the group to consider the author's comments on Paul's letters in light of these two questions: (1) What common assumptions or misconceptions about these women and their stories does the author critique?

(2) What new ways of understanding these stories do her comments suggest? Discuss as many of the author's comments as time allows.

Diving Deeper   15 minutes

Call attention to the "Diving Deeper" sections throughout this chapter and invite discussion of the author's insights about each woman, using the reflection questions that appear at the conclusion of each section. Work through as many of the questions as time allows.

Looking Further   5 minutes

"Among the persons Paul greets in Rome, nine women appear." Paul singles out several of them for comments: Prisca (and Aquila) for her work with Paul and for risking her life; Mary for her hard work; Junia as an apostle; Tryphaena, Tryphosa, and Persis for their labor. "Nothing in Paul's comments justifies the conclusion that these women worked in ways that differed either in kind or in quality from the ways in which men worked. Indeed, all of the individuals listed appear to be engaged in tasks of ministry" (Beverly Roberts Gaventa, *Women's Bible Commentary*, 555–56).

Closing

Reflect together on the biblical women from whom you've learned the most in this study.

Notes

Introduction

1. When I preach, I use the assigned texts from the Revised Common Lectionary, which is a three-year cycle of readings from the Old Testament, Gospels, Epistles, and Psalms. Often when I read the texts for a particular Sunday, my first thought is that the stories are boring and provide nothing to preach about. After a week or two of reading commentaries and digging into the text, I usually have to set aside several good possibilities in order to choose one direction for the sermon. Research has made the texts come alive.

2 Lynn Japinga, *From Widows to Warriors: Women's Stories from the Old Testament* (Louisville, KY: Westminster John Knox Press, 2020).

3. See, for example, some of the "texts of terror" in the Old Testament, such as the rape of the concubine in Judg. 19–21; the story of Jephthah's daughter in Judg. 11; the rape of Tamar in 2 Sam. 13; and many others. For more on this, see Phyllis Trible, *Texts of Terror: Literary-Feminist Readings of Biblical Narratives* (Philadelphia: Fortress Press, 1984).

4. Dorothy Sayers, *Are Women Human?* (Grand Rapids: Eerdmans, 1971), 47.

5. Melinda Gates, *The Moment of Lift* (New York: Flatiron Books, 2019), 2–3 (italics in the original).

6. Gates, *Moment of Lift*, 108–14.

7. See Brown's first TED talk, "The Power of Vulnerability," filmed in June 2010 in Houston, https://www.ted.com/talks/brene_brown_the_power_of_vulnerability, and her second TED talk, "Listening to Shame," filmed in March 2012, https://www.ted.com/talks/brene_brown_listening_to_shame. See also Brené Brown, *Daring Greatly* (New York: Gotham Books, 2012), and *Rising Strong* (New York: Spiegel & Grau, 2015).

8 Chrysostom, Homily 31 on Romans 16:6, http://www.newadvent.org/fathers/210231.htm.

Chapter 1: The Birth of Jesus

1. Some of the material in this chapter also appears in *Connections: A Lectionary Commentary for Preaching and Worship, Year B, Volume 1* (Louisville, KY: Westminster John Knox Press, 2020), commentaries for Fourth Sunday of Advent, Christmas Eve, and Christmas Day.

2. There has been significant debate in the Christian tradition about the status of Mary. The Roman Catholic doctrine of the immaculate conception says that God removed the stain of original sin from Mary before she was born. She was immaculately (without sin) conceived. Unlike the rest of humanity, Mary was sinless and pure. She had to be sinless so that she did not transmit human sin to Jesus. Protestants believe that Mary was a human being who was chosen to be the mother of Jesus not because of her credentials or virtue or purity, but simply because of God's grace and favor. Mary was a real person with real fears. She may have wished at times that God had "favored" someone else.

3. The virgin birth has been a hotly debated topic in the Christian tradition. The prophet Isaiah predicted that an *almah* would conceive and bear a son (Isa. 7:14). *Almah* can mean either a virgin or a young woman. Matthew cites this verse from Isaiah (in Matt. 1:23), and uses the Greek word *parthenos* to translate the Hebrew word *almah*. *Parthenos* has the same ambiguity and can mean either virgin or young woman. Luke also uses *parthenos* to describe Mary (1:27). Most English translations use "virgin" to translate *almah* and *parthenos* in Isaiah and Matthew. Matthew and Luke both argue that there was something unusual about Mary's pregnancy, but Mark, John, and the apostle Paul say nothing about it. The virgin birth has caused intellectual problems because it seems to insist on a biological impossibility. Some Christians have argued that Mary was either seduced or raped, and God declared her child the Son of God. Others claim that Jesus was the biological child of Joseph and Mary, and then declared to be God's Son. These proposals help to solve the biological problem, but the point of the story in both Matthew and Luke is that something unusual happens here. The conception of Jesus is miraculous. It occurs without a man. This is not a Greek or Roman myth in which a god actually has sex with a woman. Conception does not happen in the usual way of sperm-meeting-egg. The Holy Spirit will overshadow Mary and somehow she will become pregnant. It is a mystery that cannot be logically explained. In Gen. 1:1–2, God creates the world from nothing. In Luke 1, God creates a baby in Mary's empty womb.

4. See Gen. 1:2 for similar language about the wind (breath) of God as the agent of creation.

5. This raises a question about Jesus' siblings. The Roman Catholic Church argues that Mary was perpetually a virgin; the siblings of Jesus mentioned in the Bible were not Mary's children, but Joseph's children from a previous marriage, or perhaps cousins. Protestants believe that Mary and Joseph engaged in a typical sexual relationship and likely had more children after Jesus.

6. Eduard Schweizer, *The Good News according to Luke* (Atlanta: John Knox Press, 1984), 23.

7. Alice Walker, *The Temple of My Familiar* (New York: Pocket Books, 1990), 271.

Chapter 2: The Healed

1. A woman who married young, had eight to ten pregnancies, and nursed her babies between pregnancies would have had far fewer periods than the average woman today. See Anita Diamant's novel *The Red Tent* (New York: St. Martin's Press, 1997). In her fictional treatment of Dinah (Gen. 34), Diamant speculates that menstruating women might live together in a special red tent, so as not to contaminate their family members. This served as a time of female bonding and storytelling and also was a reprieve from the usual chores of cleaning and food preparation.

2. The Greek word for "save" refers to both healing the body from disease and saving the person from sin or despair or shame.

3. Rebecca Traister, *Good and Mad: The Revolutionary Power of Women's Anger* (New York: Simon & Schuster, 2018), 91–92.

4. Melinda Gates, *The Moment of Lift* (New York: Flatiron Books, 2019), 46–50.

5. Carter Heyward, *Our Passion for Justice* (New York: Pilgrim Press, 1984), 6.

6. Kate Bowler, *Everything Happens for a Reason: And Other Lies I've Loved* (New York: Random House, 2018).

7. For a discussion of cutting and family planning, see Gates, *Moment of Lift*.

8. See the Brené Brown TED talk "Listening to Shame," filmed in March 2012, https://www.ted.com/talks/brene_brown_listening_to_shame.

9. Gates, *Moment of Lift*, 105.

10. Gates, *Moment of Lift*, 53.

Chapter 3: The Outcasts

1. See *Brené Brown: The Call to Courage*, a 2019 Netflix special in which Brown explains this in more detail: https://www.netflix.com/ca/title/81010166.

2. Lewis Smedes, *Shame and Grace: Healing the Shame We Don't Deserve* (New York: HarperCollins, 1993), 126.

3. Examples of commentaries making these points can be found at https://biblehub.com/commentaries/john/4-16.htm. Unfortunately, these attitudes are not limited to the nineteenth century, but also can be found in contemporary sermons. Do an online search for "sermons on the Samaritan woman" for multiple examples. Also see "The Tragic Cost of Her Cavernous Thirst," a sermon by John Piper, https://www.desiringgod.org/messages/the-tragic-cost-of-her-cavernous-thirst.

4. Paul Duke, *Irony in the Fourth Gospel* (Atlanta: John Knox Press, 1985), 102.

5. Raymond Brown, *The Gospel according to John I–XII*, Anchor Bible (New York: Doubleday, 1966), 176, 171, 175.

6. Edith Deen, *All of the Women of the Bible* (1955; repr., San Francisco: HarperSanFrancisco, 1988), 196.

7. Pulpit Commentary on John 4:17, https://biblehub.com/commentaries/pulpit/john/4.htm.

8. See the story of Tamar and levirate marriages in Gen. 38.

9. The Roman Catholic Church developed a system of penance in part to avoid this problem of apparently easy forgiveness or cheap grace. People confessed their sins to a priest and were granted absolution; the priest also assigned prayers or actions to complete so that people could show they were really sorry for what they had done.

10. In some manuscripts, the story was inserted after Luke 21:38, in part because its language and style make it more similar to Luke's material than to John's. The story did not appear in this location in John until a fifth-century manuscript.

Chapter 4: The Grateful

1. John identifies a woman who anoints Jesus' feet as Mary of Bethany (12:1–8). See the chapter on Mary and Martha. Luke describes a "sinful" woman who anoints Jesus' feet (7:36–50), but the circumstances of that story are quite different. See the next section of this chapter.

2. *Downton Abbey,* season 3, episode 5, directed by Jeremy Webb, written by Julian Fellowes, aired January 27, 2013, on PBS.

3. It is interesting that Jesus washes the disciples' feet and no one complains that it is too intimate and sexual! Today, footwashing is an act that has sacramental status in some denominations.

4. Ruth Everhart, *Ruined: A Memoir* (Carol Stream, IL: Tyndale House, 2016), 45–46.

5. For a description of Christian spirituality that involved tearing down a person's will, intellect, desires, and emotions in order to make a new person more like Jesus, see Karen Armstrong's description of her time in a convent during the 1960s in *The Spiral Staircase: My Climb out of Darkness* (New York: Knopf, 2004), and *Through the Narrow Gate: A Memoir of Spiritual Discovery*, 2nd ed. (New York: St. Martin's Griffin, 2005).

6. Nadia Bolz-Weber, *Shameless: A Sexual Reformation* (New York: Convergent Books, 2019), 188.

7. Elizabeth Warren, *A Fighting Chance* (New York: Metropolitan Books/ Henry Holt, 2014).

Chapter 5: The Sisters

1. Roberta Bondi uses this phrase in *Memories of God: Theological Reflections on a Life* (Nashville: Abingdon Press, 1995), 44.

Chapter 6: The Cross and the Empty Tomb

1. It might be helpful to read each account of the resurrection and take note of the details. How many visitors are there? Who appears at the tomb? Where are

the disciples? When does Jesus appear? The existence of multiple stories might seem threatening to those who have been taught that the Bible is the inspired word of God. Can multiple stories all be true if their details are different? It is helpful to remember that the stories about Jesus were not formally compiled into Gospels until forty years after the death and resurrection of Jesus. The authors were not eyewitnesses, but relied on stories and memories that had been passed down.

2. These endings appear in most versions of the Bible in brackets with an explanation in the footnotes. The shorter ending is only one verse and says that the women did tell the story. The longer version includes elements mentioned in the other Gospels. Jesus appears to Mary Magdalene (as in John 20) and to two men walking with him (as in Luke 24). Also in this ending, Jesus discusses handling snakes and drinking deadly things!

3. Joel Marcus, *Mark 8–16*, Anchor Bible (New Haven, CT: Yale University Press, 2009), 1095.

4. Dan Brown, *The Da Vinci Code* (New York: Doubleday, 2003); Nikos Kazantzakis, *The Last Temptation of Christ* (New York: Bantam, 1957); Martin Scorsese directed the 1988 film version. Norman Jewison directed the 1973 film *Jesus Christ Superstar*, which was based on the 1970 rock opera by Andrew Lloyd Webber and Tim Rice.

5. Theft of a body sometimes occurred when a charismatic figure was killed and the political powers feared that his followers would set up a shrine around the burial site where they would continue to gather and promote his dangerous ideas. If the body was stolen and buried in an unmarked grave, people would not gather and his influence would be minimized.

6. Jane Schaberg, *The Resurrection of Mary Magdalene: Legends, Apocrypha, and the Christian Testament* (New York: Continuum, 2002), 68.

7. In the Getty Museum several years ago, I was disappointed to see a painting of Mary Magdalene accompanied by an explanatory card that described her as a prostitute.

8. For a helpful summary of these writings, see Bart D. Ehrman, *Peter, Paul, and Mary Magdalene: The Followers of Jesus in History and Legend* (New York: Oxford University Press, 2006).

9. Schaberg, *Resurrection of Mary Magdalene*, 91–93. See also Ehrman, *Peter, Paul, and Mary Magdalene*, 184–85.

10. This sermon, from the Requiem Eucharist for Rachel Held Evans on June 1, 2019, can be viewed on YouTube and at https://rachelheldevans.com /funeral. Bolz-Weber's sermon is from 50:25 to 1:03:50; the quotation begins at 56:29.

11. See the 2002 movie *The Magdalene Sisters*, directed by Peter Mullan.

Chapter 7: The Book of Acts

1. For an irreverent but hilarious characterization of a church lady, see Dana Carvey's "Church Lady" skits on old episodes of *Saturday Night Live*, available

on YouTube. His church lady wears a frumpy dress and hairstyle and a perfect pursed-lip judgmental expression. She is harsh and critical and shows no tolerance for the moral failings of the ministers and politicians she skewers with her trademark lines: "Is it SATAN?" "Isn't that *special*?" And "How conveeeeeenient."

2. It is possible that the author was trying to paint a positive, attractive picture of the early Christian church and to assure the Roman Empire that Christianity was not a threat. Christianity would have posed less of a threat to Roman society if women were well-behaved and busy inside the home rather than appearing in public spaces like the church.

3. Elisabeth Schüssler Fiorenza, *In Memory of Her: A Feminist Theological Reconstruction of Christian Origins* (New York: Crossroad, 1983).

4. Beverly Gaventa, *The Acts of the Apostles* (Nashville: Abingdon Press, 2003), 68.

5. Allison Vander Broek, "Prayer, Parish Life, and Spiritual Practice across Generational Divides," *Reformed Journal: The Twelve* (blog), June 29, 2019, https://blog.reformedjournal.com/2019/06/29/prayer-parish-life-and-spiritual-practice-across-generational-divides/.

6. John Winthrop, "A Modell of Christian Charity," 1630, Hanover Historical Texts Collection, https://history.hanover.edu/texts/winthmod.html.

Chapter 8: The Letters of Paul

1. Other letters in the New Testament—to the Ephesians, Colossians, Timothy, and Titus—also are attributed to Paul, but they were probably written several decades later by Paul's followers rather than by Paul himself.

2. Some commentators wonder whether Paul actually wrote these words, because they do not fit smoothly into the argument of the chapter. The other difficult passages about women's role in the church occur in 1 Tim. 2:11–12, "Let a woman learn in silence with full submission. I permit no woman to teach or to have authority over a man; she is to keep silent." And Eph. 5:22, "Wives, be subject to your husbands as you are to the Lord." Paul probably did not write these words, but they are often attributed to him.

3. Heinrich Bullinger, a Protestant reformer in the sixteenth century, claimed that Phoebe was not a minister because 1 Tim. 2 forbade women from teaching or holding office. First Timothy was probably written fifty years after Phoebe did her work. Women may have been encouraged to lead the church in 50 CE but over time their roles were constrained. Philip D. W. Krey and Peter D. S. Krey, eds., *Romans 9–16*, Reformation Commentary on Scripture, New Testament 8 (Downers Grove, IL: IVP Academic, 2016), 242.

4. Theodore Beza (1519–1605) writes that *prostatis* usually means overseer or patron, "but this name seems to be more authoritative than is fitting for a woman." He considers her a hostess who took care of guests. Krey and Krey, *Romans 9–16*, 243.

5. The website biblehub.com includes a Greek version of the New Testament with a literal translation into English. It notes that *Junia* is feminine but then calls her a "kinsman" of Paul! See https://biblehub.com/interlinear/romans/16–7.htm.

6. Gerald Bray, ed., *Romans*, Ancient Christian Commentary on Scripture, New Testament 6 (Downers Grove, IL: InterVarsity Press, 1998), 369.

7. Krey and Krey, *Romans 9–16*, 242–47.

8. Paul refers to himself as working hard for the gospel in 1 Cor. 15:10 and Gal. 4:11.

9. The author of 2 Timothy names Eunice and Lois, the mother and grandmother of Timothy, as women of sincere faith (1:5). Colossians 4:15 identifies Nympha as a leader of a house church.

10. Chrysostom, Homily 31 on Romans 16:6, http://www.newadvent.org/fathers/210231.htm.

Index of Scripture

Index of Names

CPSIA information can be obtained
at www.ICGtesting.com
Printed in the USA
LVHW081451250622
721962LV00006B/6